上海世博会博物馆 编
World Expo Museum

上海世博会博物馆
馆藏精品（一）

Precious Collection of
the World Expo Museum
Volume I

中国出版集团 东方出版中心

传承世博遗产
Passing on Expo Legacy

保存世博精髓
Preserving Expo Essence

延续世博效应
Sustaining Expo Effect

前言
Foreword

世博会是人类文明展示的大舞台，一直汇聚并呈现世界各国最新的科技、文化、艺术成果。根据惯例，为世博会所建造的建筑只有少数被保留下来，大部分都被拆除，展品也多被参展者运回。对于以往世博会的盛况，人们大多只能通过影像，而无法通过实物、实景回顾，这不免令人遗憾。

令人欣喜的是，上海世博会博物馆（以下简称"世博馆"）的建立将弥补这一遗憾。鉴于中国 2010 年上海世博会的成功，中国上海市政府与国际展览局于 2010 年 11 月合作共建了世博馆。世博馆是国际展览局官方博物馆与官方文献中心，其宗旨是传承世博遗产、保存世博精髓、延续世博效应。

为给新生的博物馆奠定藏品基础，世博馆在中国 2010 年上海世博会、韩国 2012 年丽水世博会举办期间分别开展了两次大规模的藏品和文献征集活动，得到组织者和各国参展者的大力支持与慷慨捐赠。截至 2013 年 3 月，世博馆共征集上海世博会的 219 个各国参展者和组织者无偿捐赠的 27 253 件藏品、丽水世博会的 44 个各国参展者无偿捐赠的 706 件藏品。这些藏品具有一定的历史、艺术及科学价值。

众所周知，藏品是博物馆的立馆之本，是博物馆进行陈列展览的物质基础及开展科学研究的实物资料，也是博物馆宣传推广的重要内容。正是由于这批藏品，2011 年 9 月 25 日，以"见证成功、留住精彩、延续难忘"为主题的上海世博会纪念展才能开幕。但受限于有限的展示空间，展览只能分批展示博物馆在上海世博会征集到的藏品。

为了答谢捐赠方对世博馆作出的贡献；为了让人们更全面地欣赏到这些精彩的藏品；为了克服藏品的保护和使用之间的矛盾，满足科研需要；也为了展现世博馆在藏品研究方面的学术成果，我们将有计划地、系统地将重点馆藏以图录形式，出版《上海世博会博物馆馆藏精品》系列图书，形成我馆的一个学术品牌。

本卷为第一辑。书中共收录了中国 2010 年上海世博会 146 个捐赠方捐赠的 336 件藏品。书中《世博会会期藏品征集实践及规律》一文介绍了这些藏品诞生与流传的经过及世博馆对藏品征集的学术探讨。

　　希望本书能再现世博藏品的精彩和藏品背后的难忘故事，能唤起读者对世博会的美好回忆。同样希望本书能表达世博馆对捐赠者的感激之情。作为世博印记的载体和世博情谊的纽带，这些珍贵的藏品寄托着众多捐赠者对保留世博精髓、延续世博效应的殷切期望，亦将激励我们为把世博馆打造成世博人的精神家园而孜孜不倦地努力。

　　一切始于世博会，包括友谊。藉此中国 2010 年上海世博会开幕三周年纪念之际，谨以本书献给所有为世博会博物馆倾情奉献的朋友们！

上海世博会博物馆馆长

2013 年 5 月 1 日

（中国 2010 年上海世博会开幕三周年纪念）

Foreword
前言

The World Expo is a great platform to demonstrate human civilizations, as it has always been pooling together and showcasing the latest achievements of science, technology, cultures and arts in the world. As a norm, the majority of the Expo pavilions will be demolished after the Expo, and most of the exhibits will be shipped off to their home countries by participants, with only a few Expo buildings being retained as permanent city landmarks. Hence it is regrettable yet inevitable that we can only catch a glimpse of the grandeur of previous Expos through photos and footages, instead of looking back upon them via tangible objects and live scenes.

Luckily, the World Expo Museum (Expo Museum in short) has been established in time to help us make up these regrets. In consideration of the great success of the Expo 2010 Shanghai China, the Shanghai Municipal Government and the Bureau of International Expositions (BIE) jointly founded the Expo Museum in November 2011, which is authorised as BIE's official museum and official documentation center. The Expo Museum aims to pass on the legacy, preserve the essence, and sustain the effect of the World Expo.

In an effort to lay a solid foundation for its collections, the Expo Museum launched two large campaigns to collect exhibits and archives during the Expo 2010 Shanghai China and the Expo 2012 Yeosu Korea, which won generous support and donations from the organizers and the participants. As of March 2013, the Expo Museum had collected a total of 27 253 collectibles donated by 219 participants at the Expo 2010 Shanghai China, and 706 collectibles donated from the 44 participants at the Expo 2012 Yeosu Korea. These collectibles are all of significant historical, artistic and scientific values.

As is know to all of us, a museum exists because of its collections, which are the "material base" for the museum to exhibit and the tangible objects for researchers to carry out scientific studies, as well as the content for promotion. Thanks to these collection, the Commemorative Exhibition of Expo 2010 Shanghai China, which was themed "Witnessing the Success, Retaining Splendor, and

Refreshing Memories", was able to open on September 25, 2011. The exhibition, however, could only display its collections from the Shanghai World Expo in several installments due to the space limit.

In order to express our gratitude to the donators for their contribution to the Expo Museum, to enable the public to appreciate these fantastic collections in a panoramic way, to overcome the contradiction between the preservation and utilization of the collectibles so as to cater to the research needs, and to showcase the museum's academic outcome in collection research, the Expo Museum has decided to publish a series of pictorial books, entitled Precious Collection of the World Expo Museum to introduce its precious collection in a planned and systematic way, which will help build up the academic brand of the museum.

Being the first volume of the series, this book presents 336 sets of collectibles donated by 146 participants at the Expo 2010 Shanghai China. The paper Practice and Principles in Collectibles Acquisition during World Expo in this book introduces how these collections were created, how they were transferred to the Expo Museum and the Museum's academic explorations concerning the acquisition of collectibles.

We hope this book can recreate the splendor of the Expo collectibles and help us recall the memorable stories behind them while refreshing our wonderful memories of the World Expo. We also hope that this book can convey our gratitude to the donators on behalf of the Expo Museum. As carriers of Expo impressions and bridges of Expo-related friendship, these precious collectibles embody the donators' sincere expectation to retain the Expo essences and sustain the Expo effect, which will also inspire us to make relentless effort to build the Expo Museum into a spiritual home for all the Expo people.

Everything begins with Expo, including friendship. On the occasion of the third anniversary for the opening of the Expo 2010 Shanghai China, we dedicate this book to all our friends who have made contributions to the World Expo Museum.

Director of the World Expo Museum

May 1, 2013

(In celebration of the third Anniversary for the Opening of the Expo 2010 Shanghai China)

世博会会期藏品征集实践及规律

上海世博会博物馆馆长 刘绣华

2010 年 5 月 1 日至 10 月 31 日，中国上海举办了以"城市，让生活更美好"为主题的注册类（综合性）世博会，并以参展方数量、参观人数、园区面积、服务供给的骄人纪录成为世博会历史上的里程碑。2012 年 5 月 12 日至 8 月 12 日，韩国丽水举办了以"生机勃勃的海洋与海岸"为主题的认可类（专业性）世博会。在东亚地区相继举办的这两届世博会不失为注册类和认可类世博会的成功范例，体现了亚洲国家为世界博览会事业所做的重要贡献。

鉴于上海世博会的成功，中国上海市政府及国际展览局于 2010 年 11 月合作共建了世博会博物馆（以下简称"世博馆"）。世博馆是国际展览局官方博物馆与官方文献中心，其宗旨是传承世博遗产、保存世博精髓、延续世博效应。世博馆选址于上海黄浦江畔原世博园区内，占地 4 公顷，建筑面积约 4 万平方米，预计于 2016 年建成开放，是上海市"十二五"规划期间的重大文化设施建设项目。

世博会会期展品是有形的世博遗产和宝贵的世博精髓，而藏品是博物馆陈列展览的物质基础和科学研究的实物资料，因此，世博会会期展品（藏品）可以说是筹建中的世博会博物馆的立馆之本及藏品征集的主要来源。自 2010 年 9 月起，世博馆在中国 2010 年上海世博会、韩国 2012 年丽水世博会举办期间分别开展了两次大规模的藏品和文献征集活动，得到组织者和各国参展者的大力支持与慷慨捐赠。截至 2013 年 3 月，世博馆共征集上海世博会的 219 个各国参展者和组织者无偿捐赠的 27 253 件藏品、丽水世博会的 44 个各国参展者无偿捐赠的 706 件藏品，为世博馆的发展奠定了坚实的基础。

笔者将通过介绍 2010 年上海世博会、2012 年丽水世博会这两届世博会会期藏品征集工作的实例，从世博馆分别作为组织者、参展者两种不同的定位与形式，分析世博藏品征集工作的对象、标准、规则、管理、操作及学术研究探索等规律，体现世博会会期藏品征集有别于传统博物馆面向民间藏品征集的特性，探讨文博界藏品征集的创新模式。

一、世博会会期藏品征集的特点与挑战

（一）什么是世博会？

世界博览会简称"世博会"（World Expo），它是由一个主权国家的政府主办，有多个国家或国际组织参加，以展现人类在社会、经济、文化和科技领域取得的成就的国际性大型展示会，其特点是举办时间长、展出规模大、参展国家多、影响深远，

享有"经济、科技、文化领域的奥林匹克盛会"的美誉。世博会有展示、论坛和活动三大形式[①]。

国际展览局(Bureau of International Expositions,简称 BIE)总部设在巴黎,于 1928 年依据《国际展览公约》而成立,负责规范、管理和协调世博会的举办。世博会根据性质、规模、展期不同分为两类:注册类世博会(展期 6 个月,每五年举办一次)和认可类世博会(展期 3 个月,在两届注册类世博会之间举办一次)[②]。1933 年起,每届世博会均选择一个当时人类社会共同面临和关心的、反映人类文明与社会经济发展特点或价值观追求的主题进行演绎。

中国 2010 年上海世博会是中国第一次举办的注册类(综合性)世博会。世博园区占地 5.28 平方公里,会期 184 天,参观人数 7 308 万人次,参展主体 300 多个(包括 190 个国家、56 个国际组织、18 个企业或企业联合体、中国 31 个省区市及港澳台地区、80 个各国城市案例)。会期展馆展示面积达 100 多万平方米,文化活动 2 万多场,举办了一个高峰论坛和六个主题论坛。上海世博会的组织者是"上海世博会事务协调局"(以下简称"上海世博局")[③]。

韩国 2012 年丽水世博会是认可类(专业性)世博会,位于全罗南道丽水市。世博园区占地 2.71 平方公里,展期 3 个月,共有 104 个国家和地区、10 个国际组织参展,另有 13 个海洋案例、23 个韩国地方政府、7 个企业参展。参观人数 800 万人次,展区面积 25 万平方米。组织者是"韩国 2012 年丽水世博会组委会"[④]。

(二)世博会会期藏品特点

世博会会期藏品是指组织者和参展者在其展示、活动、论坛中使用和产生的展品、纪念品和文献。世博会的性质和特点反映出世博会会期藏品有别于一般文物、藏品的特点。

1. 世博会会期藏品产生于特定主体、特定时间、特定空间

特定主体是指每届世博会数量多达一百余个甚至数百个参展者,其类别包括主权国家政府和国际组织(占大多数)、城市、企业、东道国及其地方政府。

特定时间是指世博会举办期(6 个月或 3 个月)。会期藏品征集必须在短短数月内完成,与时间赛跑是征集工作的常态。

特定空间是指世博园区物理空间的特殊性。遵照《国际展览公约》及其《关于世博会参展者进口物品的海关规章》,世博会主办国给予组织者和境外参展者在关税、工商税以及涉外税收上的优惠待遇。世博园区属于海关直接监管的保税区域,藏品进出园区受到保税区域的管理限制,藏品所有权转移(包括捐赠)涉及相关关税以及进出境手续的办理。

2. 世博会会期藏品是围绕特定主题、在特定形式中产生

世博会的展示有其独特性,是参展者围绕该届世博会主题、确定观念与题材,择取物件、通过创意形式、传递信息、以宣传教育为目的的展示。世博会每日接待观众十余万甚至数十万,展馆运营及参观服务面临小空间与大人流、短时间与多节目两个"剪刀差"的挑战。参展者往往采用具有视觉

---

①《上海世博》杂志编辑部编,《走进世博会——世博知识 150 问》,东方出版中心,2009 年。
② 国际展览局档案,《国际展览公约》。
③《上海世博会事务协调局筹备举办世博会工作总结》,上海世博会事务协调局,2010 年 12 月。
④《2012 年韩国丽水世博会官方图册》,RH Korea,2012。

冲击力的展陈形式和展品吸引走马匆匆的观众。大量创意独特的多媒体展陈形式、大体量展项、艺术装置越来越成为世博展览的趋势。世博展示有别于传统博物馆的侧重于呈现文物藏品学术内涵的以物展物的陈列展览形式。

世博藏品作为演绎主题的载体,重在呈现理念、表达故事、推广形象。它们受到众多参观者的见证与关注,发挥了广泛的宣传功能。

例如,世博馆在上海世博会接收的首件捐赠品是热门场馆西班牙馆的镇馆之宝——巨型机器人娃娃"小米宝宝"。小米宝宝由美国好莱坞著名特效制作公司为西班牙馆特制,高6.5米,重3吨,由一套复杂的电脑系统控制,其脸部、脖子和胸部能够完成十几种不同的表情。作为西班牙馆对城市主题演绎的重要展项,小米宝宝作为人类未来的象征,展示了西班牙对未来城市的改进方案及对城市可持续发展的理想未来的憧憬。作为西班牙馆的友谊使者,小米宝宝成为园区最受观众欢迎的亮点展品。小米宝宝的捐赠对世博馆藏品征集工作起到了积极的示范效应和宣传效应。

3. 世博藏品的重大事件纪念价值远胜于藏品本身的历史年代价值

世博会充分展示了丰富多彩的人类社会发展成就,汇聚了全球探索世博主题理念的共同智慧,推动了各国文化、经济、科技的交流与合作,成为了人类文明的盛会。世博会也是主办国展示国家形象及国民看世界的窗口。

世博会的藏品,除少量借展的文物和艺术品,大多是为参展而特制的新展品。与年代久远的传统文物以古旧价值为珍有所不同,世博藏品的外延价值远胜于物品本身的内涵价值。它们是反映世博会这一国际盛事和重大历史事件的典型物证,是见证成功、留住精彩、延续难忘的具象载体,具有直接见证意义和重要佐证意义,具有典型性,现存稀少,其流传经过多有特殊情节。

例如,世博馆收藏了一份珍贵文献"中国2010年上海世界博览会运行日报第184期",由园区运行指挥中心在2010年10月31日(世博闭幕日)编制。与之前183期的日报一样,该文件记载了当日世博园区运行的客流情况、运行保障情况(含交通保障、设备保障、参观者服务、物流保障、餐饮服务、志愿者活动)、活动与接待情况、安全保卫情况等常规运行工作资料。但是这份日报具有非常特殊的印记。一是文件的封面有时任上海市长韩正(上海世博会执委会主任、主运行指挥部总指挥)、时任上海市常务副市长杨雄(上海

上海世博会纪念展内"一级指挥平台"场景

中国2010年上海世界博览会运行日报第184期

世博会执委会常任副主任、主运行指挥部常任副总指挥）两位领导的签名。两位领导在 11 月 1 日 0:55 分到运行指挥中心听取闭幕日运行工作汇报，慰问中心全体工作人员，并应邀在最后一份日报上签名留念。二是该日志附有一页"见证说明"："全世界各参展方和组织者全体工作人员历经 184 天的共同努力，于 2010 年 10 月 31 日 24:00 成功完成运行任务，圆满闭幕。""这份运行日报是中国 2010 年上海世博会成功运行的珍贵文物，特送世博会博物馆（筹）收藏。"当日在中心值班的指挥长、安保指挥、应急指挥、片区/场馆指挥、信息综合等六位同志签名见证。

薄薄四页纸的文件产生于特殊背景，见证了中国经历百年梦想、十年努力、八年筹办、半年精彩取得世博会最终胜利的辉煌，见证了众多世博人在幕后为园区台前精彩所做的艰苦努力及科学运营的成果。它是对重大历史事件的反映和具有特殊纪念意义的藏品。按照国家文物局颁布的《近现代一级文物藏品定级标准（试行）》对文献、手稿类文物的说明，这份仅有两年历史的文献符合近现代一级文物藏品的定级标准[1]。

4. 世博藏品具有价值不确定性及资金来源独特性

世博藏品是以展品形式出现，材质和类型庞杂，不少物品的海关申报价格与整体展项融合在一起，难以拆分估算。世博会以官方参展者为主，绝大多数参展者（企业馆外）的参展经费由国家或地区政府、国际机构承担及筹措。在征集活动中，参展者较少考虑商业运作或商业回报，这是征集工作的优势之一。

（三）世博会会期藏品征集的特点

根据世博藏品的特点，在会期征集工作开始时，世博馆就确定了以参展者的无偿捐赠作为唯一的征集手段。一是坚持勤俭办博，二是节约关税，三是由于藏品量大、类杂且成本证据不确定，缺乏价格评估的条件和资源。四是涉外多边谈判中必须保持中立平衡的统一口径，防止个别利益方索报。这些为征集工作带来极大的挑战。

作为超大型国际性博览会，世博会举办过程中既要遵循《国际展览公约》的各项规则，又要遵守举办国内与参展品紧密相关的财税、海关、捐赠、知识产权、参展管理等系列法规法令。在世博会会期开展藏品征集活动，必须综合考量世博馆学术研究特点、参展者的沟通动员、组织者的法律框架、征集操作与世博园区管理限制等各种因素，其藏品征集模式有别于一般博物馆面向民间的藏品征集活动。下文以实例做具体阐述。

二、世博会会期藏品征集实践

（一）展览调研，确定标准与对象

在世博会开幕前，上海世博局已计划在世博会后一周年举办"上海世博会纪念展"，以延续世博后续宣传效应。笔者当时担任上海世博局新闻宣传部副部长，负责海内外沟通推介，包括世博纪念

展的筹备工作。

1. 展览未动，内容先行——园区展览调研

纪念展策展初期的要务就是收集和整理全景式反映世博会举办情况的资料素材。为此，成立调研工作组开展工作，制定了周密的园区展览调研工

① 国家文物局网站"政策法规——规范性文件"，2007 年 10 月 28 日，www.sach.gov.cn。

作方案，规范了调研操作与成果的对象与标准。

　　调研有三个目的。（1）记录。按时间空间维度，全方位多角度全程记录所有参展方、展点的展示、活动、公共景观设施及服务点。（2）汇总。按业务板块综合世博的总结性、评估性、旁站式检审资料。（3）分析。按展览项目要素制订分析评估报告，对主要项目要素及项目执行提出建议。其中各展馆亮点展品和展项是重点调研的内容。

　　调研对象力求全覆盖。按照主办方场馆、自建馆、租赁馆、联合馆、特殊展馆、地标建筑等分类，

调研组统计出园区共有 400 个展点，按物理空间（园区各片区）划分而由调研组成员分片包干完成。每个对象（展点）的调研成果包括：场馆调研表、宣传资料、图片资料文件包、拟留用实物展品及展馆内多媒体展项的记录。最核心的"场馆调研表"内容包括：（1）基础信息：展馆基本要素与技术数据、团队资料、展馆概述、建筑亮点等。（2）展示内容：按展馆展示区域划分描述内容、形式、亮点。（3）多媒体展项：内容及技术。（4）亮点展品：类型、名称、描述与尺寸。（5）活动与仪式。（6）提供素材。

2010 年上海世博会德国馆场馆调研表

编号：C1NS064　　　　　　　　　　　　　　　　　　　　　　调研日期：2010 年 5 月 19 日

德 国 馆调研表（已完成）

<table>
<tr><td rowspan="9">基础信息</td><td>别　名</td><td>无</td><td>位　置</td><td colspan="2">C 片区
塘子泾路和博成路口</td><td>邻馆</td><td colspan="2">法国馆、波兰馆</td></tr>
<tr><td>吉祥物</td><td>无</td><td>主　题</td><td colspan="2">和谐都市</td><td>网站</td><td colspan="2">www.expo2010-germany.cn</td></tr>
<tr><td>总代表</td><td>迪特马尔·施米茨</td><td>馆　长</td><td colspan="2">费熙婷</td><td>国家馆日</td><td colspan="2">5 月 19 日</td></tr>
<tr><td>建筑面积</td><td>6 000 平方米</td><td>展示面积</td><td colspan="2">3 600 平方米</td><td>投资额</td><td colspan="2">5 000 万欧元</td></tr>
<tr><td>设计师 / 团队</td><td>建筑：石凯建筑设计有限公司
展览：米拉联合设计策划有限公司</td><td>运营团队</td><td colspan="2">科隆博览会国际有限公司（执行机构）</td><td>布展团队</td><td colspan="2">胡特的努施力（德国）有限公司</td></tr>
<tr><td>展馆联系人</td><td>Ms ZHENG Lu</td><td>联系方式</td><td colspan="2">20228133
13601947459</td><td>电子信箱</td><td colspan="2">l.zheng@expo2010-germany.de</td></tr>
<tr><td>建筑亮点</td><td colspan="7">悬浮于空中的建筑</td></tr>
<tr><td>展示概述</td><td colspan="7">一座在求新与保留、创新与传统、城市与自然、集体与个人、工作与休闲、全球化与民族化之间争取平衡、求得和谐的城市。"和谐"与"都市"这两个词的组合，恰好紧扣着世博会的主题"城市，让生活更美好"。
在德国馆内，参观者可以看到来自德国经济、科研和发展的角度为日益增多的城市问题提出的解决方案：例如展馆外壁使用的银色薄膜为灵活、轻便、高反射率的光透材料，白天可减少紫外线照射，夜间可用作灯笼。参观者如同置身于一个真实的城市一般，经过起落有致的坡型景区，穿过隧道，途径规划室、花园、工厂和城市广场，最终到达和谐之旅的终点——城市能源中心。</td></tr>
</table>

<table>
<tr><td rowspan="4">展馆展示</td><td>展　区</td><td>位置 / 环境</td><td>内　容</td><td>亮　点</td><td>形式及技术</td><td>感　受</td></tr>
<tr><td>排队系统</td><td>德国馆外周边</td><td>排队走线：约 1 000 米
排队时间：约 60 分钟
人流控制：60 人 / 分钟</td><td></td><td>遮阳棚及栏杆
共分 4 段，每段折回 3-5 排</td><td>1. 排队时间较长
2. 排队过程枯燥，无任何展项</td></tr>
<tr><td>风　景</td><td>户外展区
位于草坪下方</td><td>可漫步其间的坡状景园。路边竖立着严思写给燕燕的巨幅三维明信片。这些明信片展现了德国的自然风光与名胜古迹，譬如萨克森州的易北砂岩山脉，勃兰登堡门，以及新天鹅堡。</td><td>可供拍照的立体风景图片</td><td>风景背板实物模型</td><td>观众可在图片前拍照留念，同时可以消磨令人烦恼的等待时间（趣味互动）。
舒缓观众在排队等候期附带不良情绪。</td></tr>
<tr><td>隧　道</td><td>户外转向室内二楼</td><td>应用多媒体效果设计的场景将参观者带入城市图像和音效的海洋中：火车、汽车、公共汽车、行人与踩滑板的人从参观者身边经过。</td><td></td><td>电动滚梯</td><td>1. 减少步行距离、舒缓脚部压力
2. 展厅蓝色基调，平稳参观者心情
3. 调整参观节奏</td></tr>
</table>

（续表）

	展区	位置/环境	内容	亮点	形式及技术	感受
展馆展示	规划室	室内展厅三楼空间展厅主体1	这个展厅的主题是关于创新和可持续性的城市发展和城市基础设施建设。		大厅的地面和墙上都布满巨幅设计图、建筑模型、设计草图和城区规划图	优点：设计方式简单、讨巧、有立体感 缺点：走线较散、展项关联性小，部分展项设计有缺陷、存在危险隐患
	花园	室内展厅三楼空间展厅主体2	这里展示着德国绿地建设的几个典型类型：小果园、学校庭院，还有如跨文化园这样的可持续性园林。孩子们可以从这里乘滑梯滑向下一个展厅。		由图片、仿声和三维空间的展品组成	优点：有趣味性、互动性 缺点：互动展项过于集中，人流参观停滞
	储藏室	室内展厅三楼空间展厅主体2	这是一个木质感的大房间。在高至屋顶的大架子上，陈列着许多著名的发明和设计产品。它们在改善城市的生活中起着重要的作用，展品丰富。		德国制造展品及设计汇总	展台设计独特 （展品全封闭保护）
	工厂	室内展厅三楼空间展厅主体2	这间大厅中的一切都在不停地运动。参观者在这里乘滚动电梯前行，在他们的上方，传输带穿梭往来于不同层面的展品之间。		电动滚梯 吊顶展项 （仿工厂流水线） 感应操作展项 （互动展项）	过渡空间、有趣味性 在互动中了解科技
	城市广场	室内展厅三楼空间展厅主体3	城市广场是和谐都市的中心；它是城市居民聚集交流的地方，它为居民的集体活动、相互交流和自由发表言论提供了一个场所。各种文化和各年龄层的人们在这里相遇、交流、举办活动。这里也是文化和艺术的舞台。 多媒体影厅：在振动幕墙上，投射德国都市生活。		多媒体影厅"D"形投影幕	注重细节，参观者进入影厅将发现，白色物体发射荧光，增加趣味性。
	动力之源	室内展厅三层空间	德国展馆的精彩亮点，也是力量和快乐的源泉。 解说员严思和燕燕邀请参观者参与互动。球体上将呈现城市愿景图，说明保护与创新同等重要，各种文化互为补充、相得益彰，不同年龄的人们相互帮助、相互支持。	参观者通过鼓掌和叫喊影响金属球体甚至整个空间，并使金属球体摆动起来。	参观者将被分散到围绕大厅的三层回廊上，大厅的中心元素：一个金属球体。它直径三米，表面安装了400 000多根发光二极管。表演时间：七分钟	优点：展项互动性高，带动观众情绪。 缺点：展项时间过长，展项等候区域及散场通道设计存在隐患（应急通道与等候通道紧连，无法疏散人流）。 约10分钟表演一场，按展馆一分钟放行60人计算，10分钟约有600人需进入多媒体展厅。

	类型	展品名称	展品描述	展品尺寸	来源及出处
展品	国宝、文物	无	无	无	无
	捐赠	无	无	无	无
	特制品	黄铜片"绊脚石"	德国艺术家GUNTER DEMNIG展示的一种个人创意：在纳粹受害者生前最后居住的房屋前，将镶有黄铜片的石块铺设在人行道上，黄铜片上刻有受害者的姓名及出生和死亡的日期。这样，走在德国街头，你就会在不经意间与那段特殊的历史邂逅。	约8CM×8CM	铺设黄铜片"绊脚石"没有任何来自官方的资助，完全通过民间捐款来完成。所有受害者的亲属只要出资95欧元就可以铺设这样的一块石头。
	建筑结构	银色薄膜	灵活、轻便、高反射率的光透材料，白天可减少紫外线照射，夜间可用作灯蓬。		
	特色物品	储藏室墙面	储藏室展区内整个墙面陈列着许多著名的发明和设计产品。整面墙体都可以称为德国制造的代表作。		

活动及仪式	国家馆日	演出场馆：世博轴阳光谷 演出团体：欧洲青年交响乐团，"柏林总部"嘻哈乐队、"两居室"流行乐队 节目简介："欧洲青年交响乐团"将演奏莫扎特的小夜曲，德国嘻哈乐队－柏林总部将演奏节奏音乐口技和嘻哈，德国乐队"两居室"将为观众带来最新流行乐曲
	平日活动	上海世博会期间，德国16个联邦州将在位于展馆入口区域的联邦州通道展示自己的地方特色。
	仪式及其他	5月19日，上海世博会德国国家馆日官方仪式在世博中心举行。德国总统霍斯特克勒，中共中央政治局委员、上海市委书记俞正声出席仪式并致辞。霍斯特·克勒总统和夫人埃娃·露易斯·克勒饶有兴趣地亲身体验展示德国风情的多媒体装置。此外，霍斯特·克勒总统还为参观上海世博会的德国小朋友签名留念。

备注	工作团队人数：450人；解说员：250人 优点：展品及互动展项较多、趣味性强，展项丰富。参观节奏控制较好，多处展厅设计可安抚游客情绪。 缺点：展项太多太散。

上海世博会 400 个展点的调研成果构成了庞大的资料库。韩国丽水世博会的展馆调研历时 3 个月，分批派遣赴韩工作的廿余名工作人员完成了所有 166 个展点的调研，拍摄与收集了 6 万余张图片及大量视频资料。

海量而扎实的调研内容催生了可征集藏品的清单、藏品与演绎内容分析、视觉形态素材、联络对象、技术参数。调研实现了全方位记录各展馆信息、多角度表现各展点展示形态的目的；同时也有利于预判藏品征集的工作量及人财物等资源配置、测算撤展——包装——运输——仓储等操作需求。调研同时兼顾了学术研究和项目操作指引的目的。

2. 资料建库，海中定针——展点编码系统

由于调研内容海量、操作人员多且交叉或有更替，为建档、查询、统计的规范性和持续性，调研小组创立了一套"上海世博会展点编码系统"。展馆按官方认可的参展者名单排序，每个展点配备一个由 5 级共 7 位字符组成的独特编码，分别代表该展点所处位置（片区）、参展性质、参展类别、场馆类型及展点编号。例如：中国馆编码"A2US001"（A 片区——主办方——主办方展馆——自建馆——001 号），利物浦案例馆编码"E1UJ297"（E 片区——参展方——城市实践区案例——联合馆——297 号）。此编码用于征集工

2010 年上海世博会展点编码结构说明

第一级	第二级	第三级	第四级	第五级
A 片区		N 参展国家	S 自建馆	中国馆 001
		O 国际组织		参展国家 002-190
B 片区				国际组织 191-246
	1 参展方	C 企业馆	L 租赁馆	企业 247-264
		U UBPA		UBPA 265-343
C 片区				省区市馆 344-374
	2 主办方	H 主办方场馆	J 联合馆	主题馆 375-379
				世博会博物馆 380
D 片区		F 配套设施		生命阳光馆 381
				公众参与馆 382
				新能源展示厅 383
E 片区		E 特 殊	P 公共地标	世博中心 384
				世博轴 385
				世博文化中心 386
				宝钢大舞台 387
				综艺大厅 388
				三大公园 389-391
				非洲联合馆结构及外形 392
				园区交通 393
				园区雕塑 394
				园区指示牌 395
				港、澳、台 396-398
				BIE 展览 399
				塔希提岛 400

备注：
世博园区展点编码标识由 5 级编码共 7 位字符组成。
第一级：由 1 位字符组成（字符为：A、B、C、D、E），分别代表世博园区围栏区内各片区；
第二级：由 1 位字符组成（字符为：1、2），分别代表参展性质；
第三级：由 1 位字符组成（字符为：N、O、C、U、H、F、E），分别代表参展类别；
第四级：由 1 位字符组成（字符为：S、L、J、P），分别代表场馆类型；
第五级：由 3 位数字组成（字符为：001-400），分别代表展点编号。

编号原则：
1. 根据国际参展部：关于印发《上海世博会参展国家和国际组织排序名单》的通知（以下简称：通知），对在该通知中所列国家及国际组织按顺序依次编码，即 001-246；
2. 所有展点编码无重复，自 001-400，除国际参展部公布的官方排序外，其余参展方及地标排序均参照《官方导览手册》及 D、E 片区部公布的排列顺序，特殊案例放在所有展点最后体现。

例 如：
中国馆 A2US001 、天津馆 A2UJ345 、台湾馆 A2ES398 、足迹馆 E2HS378、白莲泾公园 A2FP389
UBPA 澳门案例（1 类案例）E1US269 、UBPA 利物浦案例（2 类案例）E1UJ297

作的全过程，也适用于以后纪念展的展陈大纲素材、博物馆的藏品清册记录、文献资料库查询。在2012年韩国丽水世博会的调研中，由于展馆类型简单且数量较少，编码被简化成二级四位字符的编码（按照展馆类别和展馆序号）。

可以发现此编码系统侧重于按同一届世博会期间藏品来源展馆的类别划分，有别于常规博物馆的藏品信息分类代码。随着世博馆近两年增加了世博历史藏品和办博单位纪念物的征集，藏品来源、年代、类别日趋多样化；同时随着藏品库房和信息化管理的逐渐细化，结合博物馆登记、录入、定级等行业常规操作的特点，目前正在编制另一套侧重于按材质、年代分类的藏品编码系统。具体操作中采用双码互相印证的模式。

3. 执行未启，标准先定——藏品征集工作方案

上海世博会会期藏品征集分为办博单位办博纪念物和参展者实物展品及档案资料两类。其中第一类的操作模式是由上海世博会执委会发文致各官方办博单位予以征集，以行政手段为主，本文不予阐述。

上海世博局作为官方组织者，面向所有参展者征集实物展品及档案。实物展品要求是在世博展馆内展出或使用，引起广泛关注，具有代表性、唯一性、创意性或重要纪念价值的实物展品，具体分六类：

A. 展馆象征：引起广大关注、可作为展馆象征符号的展品（镇馆之宝）。如：象征英国馆"种子圣殿"展示的蕴含植物种子的透明亚克力杆。

B. 特制品／首发品：为上海世博会特制、有创新或首次使用的展品。如：韩国馆由韩、中艺术家共同设计制作的古铜钱树"金兰之交"。

C. 高科技／新材料：有较高科技含量、使用新材料，并有较高纪念价值的展品。如：通用汽车馆的采用新能源的概念车"叶子"。

D. 国宝／文物复制品：国宝及文物特制的模型或复制品。如：埃塞俄比亚馆的首个直立行走人类骸骨"露西"复制件（原件保存在埃塞俄比亚国家博物馆，全球仅5个复制件）。

E. 其他：设计独特，可生动演绎城市主题的展品。如：城市未来馆"城市剪影"大型雕塑。

F. 纪念品：重大活动、重要人物、重要节点使用过的有特殊纪念价值的物品。如：万科馆的由万科集团董事长王石带上珠穆朗玛峰的世博会旗。

征集要求所提供的实物展品无产权纠纷，属于参展者有权处理的展品。鉴于保管维护与操作性原因，不接收国宝与文物展品，不接收活体动物、植物和食品类实物展品。

与上海世博会相比，丽水世博会的参展规模较小、展示内容较少、展陈形式更多采用多媒体，因此，可征集的实物展品也相应减少许多。另一方面，由于海外操作的复杂性和艰巨性、出国参展人手和资金有限等原因，会期藏品的征集模式也相应进行了调整。所接收的实物展品分为四类：展馆广受欢迎的核心展品、为世博会特制或首发的展品、与主题相关的展品、突出民族性或文化独特性的展品等。为运输方便，藏品长、宽、高不超过2米。

征集工作分五个步骤推进：

（1）提交意向。各参展者填写并提交《向上海世博会博物馆提供实物展品意向表》。

（2）提交档案类资料。内容包括：展馆实际展陈情况介绍、展品介绍、宣传品、馆日及重要活动资料等。提交形式包括文档、图片、视频资料及印刷品。

（3）沟通确认。世博馆与参展者进行沟通协调，向参展者反馈确认收集实物展品；

（4）办理手续。世博馆办理相关海关、税费等手续，参展者提供相关协助（根据海关有关规定，留存展品应在复运出境、进境期限届满30日前向

主管地海关等机构申请办理相关手续）；

（5）展品移交。世博闭幕后撤展期间，参展者提交实物展品，世博馆向参展者出具收藏证书。

（二）团队架构，强化组织保障

1. 上海世博会藏品征集组织架构

2010 年 7 月，上海世博局实质性启动世博馆筹办工作。8 月，上海市政府决策，确定从"立项规划、物色场地、组织保障、尽快收集档案纪念物"四个方面快速推进世博馆（曾名"纪念馆"）筹备工作。其中搭建强有力的组织架构确保了会期藏品征集工作的高效实施。

上海世博局成立"上海世博会纪念馆筹建领导小组"，由上海市政府副秘书长、上海世博局局长洪浩同志担任领导小组组长。领导小组下设"筹建办公室"，由上海世博局副局长、上海市文物局局长朱咏雷同志担任办公室主任，笔者担任常务副主任。

筹建办工作由世博局新闻宣传部牵头，由局内 16 个部门指定人员组成跨部门工作团队，紧密合作，协同工作。工作团成员来自：新闻宣传部、国际参展部、物流中心、综合计划部（资产管理中心）、技术办公室、法律事务部、资金财务部（捐赠办）、档案室、监察审计部、AB 片区部（亚洲国家与国际组织）、C 片区部（欧美洲国家）、DE 片区部（企业馆）、城市最佳实践区部（城市案例）、非洲联合馆管理部（非洲联盟与非洲国家）、中国馆部（国家馆、省区市馆、港澳台地区馆）、主题馆部。世博局另外 29 个部门确定联络人予以配合。

国际展览局、中国国际贸易促进委员会成为藏品征集的"外援团"，前者对动员各国参展者、后者对动员中国 31 个省区市积极参与征集工作给予了指导和大力支持。

到征集后期的展品征收移交工作大规模启动

时，引入了一家征收移交项目服务商和三家（世博园区指定）物流服务商。征集工作团队扩充到 200多人，分为 8 个工作小组（7 个片区组和 1 个特殊展项组）进入园区工作。

2. 丽水世博会藏品征收组织架构

2011 年初，上海世博会博物馆正式成立，笔者担任馆长。世博馆的展陈管理部负责藏品的征集与管理工作。

作为国展局官方博物馆，世博馆设计、制作了"国际展览局世博会历史巡回展"。2012 年 5 月至 8 月，该展首次在韩国丽水世博会的国展局馆展出。世博馆以参展者的身份，在丽水世博会成功完成了国展局馆运营、园区调研、藏品征集、学术研讨、宣传推广等系列工作。

如果说，在上海世博会征集藏品，世博馆是以组织者的身份"主场作战"的话，到了丽水世博会，世博馆则是以参展者的身份赴海外"客场迎战"而开展藏品征集活动，困难重重，组织保障更显重要。

在机构层面，确定了国展局馆由国际展览局、上海市政府、丽水世博会组委会三家共同主办、世博馆承办的组织架构。在工作层面，世博馆分七批次共派遣二十余名工作人员赴丽水工作。在技术层面，国展局指定的德国物流服务商和世博馆委托的上海展览服务商、物流服务商参与了藏品征收工作。

（三）特殊规章，夯实法律框架

参展者展品征集涉及不少政策条例。为此，征集工作组与法务专家认真研究规则及其操作流程，与主管部门积极沟通，结合征集工作的需要和参展者普遍关注的问题，制定或推动出台了数个法令文件。

1. 关于财税政策规范

《国际展览公约》中《关于国际展览会参展

者进口物品的海关规章》第三条规定：直接用于展览和演示的货物、外国展品的展示中使用的货物，按暂准进口规定办理，并且展会结束后复运出境的，免征进口关税和间接税[1]。

按照以上规定，中国政府制定了上海世博会财税支持政策。2005 年 12 月 7 日，财政部发出《财政部〈关于 2010 年上海世界博览会进口税收政策问题的函〉》（财关税函（2005）第 22 号）；2006 年 1 月 4 日，海关总署发出《海关总署〈关于 2010 年上海世界博览会进口税收政策有关问题的通知〉》（署税发（2006）第 3 号）。以上两份文件的第一条规定："对上海世博会事务协调局取得的来自外国政府、国际组织无偿捐赠的用于世博会的进口物资，免征关税和进口环节增值税、消费税[2]。"

世博会期间，海关派员在世博园区内驻场监管，办理海关手续。根据海关《中国 2010 年上海世博会物资通关须知》对捐赠物资免税进境的规定："外国政府、国际组织无偿捐赠给世博局的用于世博会的进口物资，由世博局向海关提出书面申请，同时提交捐赠国政府或国际组织的赠送函、由国家有关主管部门出具的'外国政府、国际组织无偿赠送及我国履行国际条约进口物资证明'和进口物资清单。海关对符合以上条件的进口物资免征关税和进口环节增值税、消费税[3]。"

按照世博会的法务规则，组织者通过制定《一般规章》、《特殊规章》、《参展指南》、《撤展指南》等一系列法律文件，向参展者具体阐述政府的相关政策、组织者对参展和运营管理的相关规定、以及具体操作指引。在上海世博局颁布的《上海世博会特殊规章第 7 号——有关货物的通关、运输和处理》，第四章第二十五条"境外捐赠的物品"中，在捐赠品免税政策和通关操作的章节对海关规定作了具体说明[4]。

2. 关于向世博馆捐赠展品的相关规定

为支持世博馆藏品征收工作，上海世博局制定了以下法令：

（1）2010 年 9 月 8 日，向各参展者发出《关于为上海世博会纪念馆收集参展者档案资料和实物展品的通知》，说明了收集对象、收集内容、有关要求、提供实物展品的回报、推进时间等。

（2）2010 年 10 月颁发的《中国 2010 年上海世界博览会参展者展馆撤展和拆除工作指南》第 5 号文件——《关于参展者物资后续处置所涉关税、许可证件和检验检疫手续的规定》中，"捐赠"条款中特别规定："组织者将在世博会闭幕后建设上海世博会纪念馆，参展者将其展览品或免税进境货物捐赠给组织者用于上海世博会纪念馆的，可免征关税和进口环节增值税。"

（3）《展馆撤展与拆除工作指南》第 17 号文——《关于参展者向上海世博会纪念馆捐赠展品移交流程的规定》，说明了实物展品捐赠所涉及的提交捐赠申请和实物展品移交流程，说明了展品移交工作团的人员证件和包装箱识别以及办理进境展品的免税、进口许可证件及检验检疫手续[5]。

（4）捐赠品免税及核销手续

由于上海世博会期征集时世博馆尚未建立机构，无法办理免税手续。经与海关总署申请，此特殊情况得到海关总署的支持。2011 年 3 月 21 日，海关总署发函上海市人民政府：《海关总署关于上海世博会博物馆（筹）接受捐赠展品有关问题的意

---

① 国际展览局资料，《国际展览公约》。
② 吴云飞主编，《上海世博会财经纪事》，上海财经大学出版社，2012 年 10 月。
③ 上海世博会事务协调局，《中国 2010 年上海世界博览会规范性文件汇编》，2010 年 12 月。
④ 上海世博会事务协调局，《中国 2010 年上海世界博览会规范性文件汇编》，2010 年 12 月。
⑤ 上海世博局，《中国 2010 年上海世界博览会参展者展馆撤展和拆除工作指南》，2010 年。

见》(署税函【2011】157号)^①，其中说明："我署原则同意在上海世博会博物馆正式建制之前，由上海世博局代替上海世博会博物馆作为受赠单位办理接受上海世博会境外官方参展者捐赠进境展品的相关免税手续。待上海世博会博物馆正式成立后，上海世博局应及时将有关免税进境捐赠展品移交给上海世博会博物馆，并同时向上海海关申请办理相关手续。"文件同时对免税手续作了适当简化。

在世博馆正式注册成立并办妥免税手续之前，所征集藏品存放于世博园区的免税物流仓库，受海关监管。一年半以后，所有捐赠品物权移交及免税核销手续办结，藏品从上海世博局整体划拨世博馆，藏品从世博园区迁往世博馆新库房。

正是在各个行政及法务主管部门"寓服务于管理"的法律保障下，藏品征集工作组得以依法合规、务实高效地推进工作。

专题协调上海世博会展品征集的海关检疫检验工作

2010年上海世博会，西班牙馆捐赠展品洽谈会议

（四）沟通募集，专业功业敬业

藏品征集的目标是"物"，但征集过程重要的是做"人"的工作。良好的沟通是募集能否成功的关键。

根据世博会规则，每个参展者任命一名展区总代表（国家馆的"政府总代表"、其他展馆的"展馆代表"或"馆长"），负责组织本展馆参展事务以及与组织者联系。此展区总代表有权代表参展者处置展品（藏品），他们是征集工作的主要沟通对象。

展区总代表推举出指导委员会成员数十名，成为"展区总代表联席会议指导委员会"。指导委员会职责是：负责在世博会的日常管理中，代表所有官方参展者的共同利益，与组织者沟通、决议重要参展工作事宜^②。指导委员会每月召开一次会议，该会议是世博馆对藏品征集工作进行沟通、推广的

重要平台。此外，国际展览局、中国馆代表也在会议上表态支持世博馆征集工作，给予参展者积极影响。

2010年9月24日，上海世博局在第七次指导委员会上介绍了筹建世博馆及征集展品的计划，很快引起众多参展者的关注与反馈。2012年6月，世博馆代表参加了丽水世博会的指导委员会会议，推介展品募集工作。2012年7月23日，世博馆在丽水举办"世博遗产的传承、研究和利用"国际研讨会，120余位近几届世博会组织者和丽水参展者代表出席，成为丽水世博会规格最高的研讨会。世博馆在会上介绍了对上海世博会捐赠藏品的保护、宣传和利用的情况，在丽水募集展品的意向和操作指引，激发了参展者对征集的积极回应。

除了专题会议介绍之外，募集工作更多是靠在日常工作中与参展者直接面对面、针对具体展品、围绕关注和难点、解决个案操作的大量工作沟

① 上海世博局档案，2011年。
② 上海世博局编，《中国2010年上海世博会法律规范汇编》，2010年4月。

通。工作组对征集可能涉及的原则性、政策性和操作性问题逐一排查，梳理出"捐赠藏品常见问题应答口径"，在沟通中释疑解惑、加深了解、回应捐赠者的诉求。对参展者共同关注的难点问题，进行专题协调，尽量为参展者提供服务、提供方便，调动其赠送展品的积极性与荣誉感。在前期调研的基础上，征集小组整理出"园区可征集展品清单"、"精选征集展品清单"（100件）、"重点征集展品清单"（20件），在全面募集捐赠品时，也组成专门谈判小组，有的放矢地争取重点展品。

事在人为。在征集人员专业敬业的努力下，精诚所至，金石为开，参展者纷纷慷慨捐赠，一些重点展品陆续落实。两次世博会期征集活动取得了数量上和质量上的丰收。

（五）征集实施，项目管理与执行

藏品征收和移交阶段临近世博会后期，正是所有参展者展馆撤展、展品回运、人员撤离最繁忙的时候，也是组织者受理物流、报关、核销、出入园等各环节手续最密集、压力最大之时，整个世博园区是个通宵加班的大工地。这些都增加了展品征集的紧迫感和操作难度。

2010年11月1日至12月31日，捐赠展品征收和移交工作在整个世博园区全面铺开。这是一个短时间、大面积、大体量，多主体、多环节、立体交叉作业的大型项目，具有以下特点：

工作对象多（106个展馆、约200个参展者）；作业面广（3.28平方公里的世博园围栏区内、跨越黄浦江两岸）；操作时间紧（2个月撤展期限内、大量集中在11月上旬移交）；投入人力多（世博局员工30余人、服务商200人、物流商3家，分为7个片区组和1个特殊展项组）；物品种类庞杂（1万多件，包括众多大体量装置、雕塑、展项需拆卸包装运输）；物流需求大（5千平方米保税仓、200平方米户外堆场、4个临时打包点约2000平方米、货运量大）；管理条线交叉（涉及世博局16个管理部门及海关、检验检疫部门手续）；操作环节多（包括信息发布与反馈、组织保障、后勤

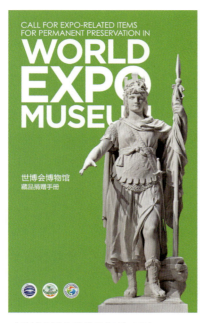

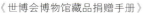

《世博会博物馆藏品捐赠手册》

2012年丽水世博会，突尼斯馆向世博会博物馆捐赠马赛克画"海洋之神"

2010 年上海世博会，西班牙馆"小米宝宝"捐赠仪式

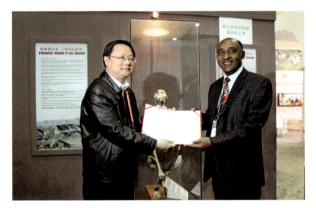

2010 年上海世博会，埃塞俄比亚馆展品捐赠仪式

2012 年丽水世博会，西班牙馆与世博会博物馆签署展品捐赠协议

保障、展品征收和移交、海关及检验检疫手续、后续事宜六大板块 23 个子项目的任务）；安全责任重（价值高、工地施工管理、消防压力等）。

经过周密计划、统一标准、任务分解，经过沟通协调、突破难点、快速反应，形成了有力指挥、

环节畅通、快速反应、现场解决的工作机制。在征集工作组、捐赠者、服务商、园区管理部门的紧密配合下，短短两个月之内保时、保量、保质地落实了近 2 万件捐赠品的移交工作，确保了藏品征集工作的成果。

（六）宣传回报，为求源头活水来

世博馆给予捐赠者的回报包括：收藏证书、在展览及对外推广中享有署名权、宣传册刊名纪念、举行仪式、媒体报道等多种形式。

2010 年 10 月 25 日，世博馆获赠首件展品——西班牙馆小米宝宝，在西班牙馆举行捐赠仪式。西班牙副首相爱莲娜·塞孔达，上海市政府副秘书长、上海世博局局长洪浩出席捐赠仪式。"'小米宝宝'留在上海了"成为热点新闻被海内外媒体广泛报道，得到各届人士的高度关注，其宣传效应也鼓励了更多参展者捐赠展品。

对捐赠者更好的宣传回报是长期展示。2011年 9 月 25 日起，世博馆举办了"上海世博会纪念展"。该展览位于原世博园区，展馆 2 万平方米，回顾了 2010 年上海世博会的举办盛况及筹备、举办世博会的情况，是"浓缩世博精华的小世博会"。近 2 900 件各国参展者捐赠的藏品在纪念展展出，唤起了观众对世博会的美好回忆。展览获得"上海市博物馆陈列展览精品奖"，开幕至今已接待近 60 万观众和近千名各国贵宾，举办十余次大型推广活动，各类报刊陆续发表了 500 余篇、40 余万字的相关报道，网络媒体和世博馆官方网站、官方微博持续发布信息，极大推广了世博馆和上海世博之城形象。纪念展还成为世博国际大家庭的一个长期的"精神家园"，许多上海世博会参展者来纪念展参观交流，一些参展者至今仍陆续捐赠展品和文献资料，体现了世博情谊的绵延不断。

2013 年 5 月 18 日至 8 月 31 日，世博馆将在

上海举办"海洋，万物的乐园——2012 年韩国丽水世博会回顾展"。丽水世博会参展者捐赠的数百件藏品将在此展出，原丽水世博会组委会嘉宾将应邀前来上海参观展览、探讨合作。此外，世博馆近年陆续出版了《成功、精彩、难忘——上海世博会纪念展》、《丽水世博会系列丛书》、《上海世博会博物馆馆藏精品》，体现对捐赠者的宣传回馈，鼓励未来捐赠。

2010 年上海世博会，西班牙馆"小米宝宝"和广东馆"瓷板画"移交现场

世博会博物馆藏品管理仓库

藏品的拍摄与维护工作

2010 年上海世博会纪念展布展现场

上海世博会纪念展

上海世博会纪念展内，"小米宝宝与蔚蓝星空"展项

三、启　迪

在世博会会期藏品征集经验的基础上，结合世博馆筹建的情况，笔者有以下思考，希望抛砖引玉，求教于各界文博专家。

（一）创建体系，形成特色，是世博馆筹建与发展的指导原则

世博会会期藏品征集情况特殊、没有先例。世博馆边做边学，摸索出一些规律，并逐渐形成适合自身需要、具有自身特色的理论及操作模式。从展览调研与分析、藏品选择标准与特色、编码分类系统，到项目管理与操作、法律规则与保障、整合营销推广等，都讲求实效、另辟蹊径、自成体系。

工作推进中，单体做实注重"本体论"，整体集成讲究"系统论"，统筹兼顾定性与定量、重点与全局、内容与渠道、理论与实际、研究与执行等因素。"理清事、找对人、走对路、成善果。"这些在实践中摸索创建的体系，力求"内容研究横向到边，项目推进纵向到底"，成为指导藏品征集工作的关键。

正如中国是首次举办世博会，世博馆作为全球唯一的世博会博物馆和中国首家真正意义上的国际性博物馆，其建设没有现成经验可借鉴，无可依循的发展模式。在新馆筹建打基础之时，无论是藏品征集、展陈策划、学科研究、社会教育、国际交流等功能与定位，均应结合实际形成自身特色。

作为从世博往文博转型的新兵，一方面要虚心学习海内外优秀博物馆的经验，另一方面也可突破条框限制，务实创新，探索一条结合世博与文博特色、适应自身需要的未来发展道路。一届成功、精彩、难忘的世博会需要催生一个成功、精彩、难忘的世博会博物馆。学习实干是成功的基础、开拓创新是精彩的驱动、鲜明特色是难忘的关键。这理应成为世博人矢志追求的使命。

（二）注重研究，整合藏品——研究——展陈业务，是世博馆学术软实力培养的关键

博物馆筹建时往往忙于工程建设，但"软件"的建设不应被忽略。优秀的博物馆应着力于发展各种高端展览、社会教育、学术研究与国际交流等专业实力的"软件"，而非过于依赖建筑物外观标新立异与视觉效果的"硬件"。其中扎实的学术研究，是众多业务拓展的知识基础和长期可持续发展的源源动力。

世博藏品征集之所以成功，是因为所有的项目策划与操作设计是根植于扎实的调查研究基础，而研究也指导、贯穿了藏品工作从征集、管理到展陈、出版的整个"产业链"。一方面各业务要善于利用研究资源，由内容决定形式；另一方面，研究也要结合各业务的特点和需求，不能闭门造车。

在博物馆的三大功能：收藏、研究、展览，如果收藏是基础，展览是功用，研究工作就是解析藏品信息、指导展览之承上启下的重要环节[1]。如果把此三个功能及其业务部门整合资源、统筹管理，更能发挥互补协同优势。近期，世博馆调整管理布局，将展陈、藏品、文献研究业务职能划归同一位馆领导分管。在新馆的展陈大纲编写以及临时展览策展工作中，打破行政部门的界限，把展陈、藏品、文献研究部门的人员按项目需求和业务流程重新组合，尝试以项目制管理的模式去优化工作效能。

---

① 姚安，《博物馆12讲》，科学出版社，2011年12月。

（三）广开渠道，增加类别，充实世博馆藏品系列

世博馆刚成立两年，绝大多数藏品来自上海、丽水两届世博会，近期新增百余件世博会历史奖章、奖牌。丰富藏品的数量和类型是一项重要的任务。

扩充藏品可以从"溯古、求新、拓宽"三个方向努力。所谓"溯古"，是在海内外收集反映世博会 160 多年历史的证物。所谓"求新"，是为征集 2017 年、2020 年和未来世博会的藏品打好基础、建立机制。例如，争取国展局的支持，把组织者和参展者支持官方博物馆藏品文献收集工作纳入参展义务之一，为征集提供法律保障。加强与国际世博社区的交流，搭建平台提供服务，增加他们对世博馆的归属感。所谓"拓宽"，是指藏品不局限在世博会上亮相的展品，也可适当拓展外延，考虑与世博会同一时期、呼应世博主题的，对人类社会经济、文化重要发展和观念更新发挥关键作用的藏品，包括近现代藏品，毕竟世博藏品特点是主题演绎价值重于年代价值。

（四）注重学习，培养复合型人才，为新馆发展注入活力

在参展丽水世博会期间，因资源限制派驻韩国工作人员每批仅 4 ~ 6 人，通过多批次轮换方式让尽可能多的骨干有学习锻炼的机会。前方人员除了负责超大人流情况下的展馆开放运营之外，还同时承担园区调研、展品征集、研讨交流及媒体宣传等工作。人手少任务重，无法按人员专业划分固定岗位职能，而是按照一人多岗、一岗多能的原则，要求每个人都成为多面手。展陈部藏品管理人员负责制定征集计划和标准，前方工作组每个人都参与了展览调研、藏品分析、沟通募集及征收移交的工作，都成为复合型的藏品征集工作人员。

员工十分珍惜在丽水的学习机会，在全面记录世博"热闹"之余，还深入挖掘办博的"门道"，从专业的角度但不受自己专业限制地研究世博会。办公室行政人员分析超大型多媒体展项，藏品部员工分析二维码在展览中的运用趋势，社会教育部员工解析多媒体秀的创意理念，物业部员工分析地区展馆参展情况，国际交流员工通过客流量分析展馆运营的规律，等等。这些"不务正业"的考察报告颇有新意，也体现员工求知上进的综合素质。

世博馆员工平均年龄 36 岁，60% 有大学学历，组成一个年轻有活力、可塑性强的团队。作为新单位，世博馆暂时没有严格细分技术专业岗位或学科分类研究职能，对通才的需求多于专才。另一方面，新馆百业待兴，也提供了学习和锻炼的机会。因此，鼓励跨学科学习，尝试轮岗锻炼，培养复合型人才，为将来培养专才做好积累。要把新馆工程建设和博物馆未来发展定位的规划相结合，把筹建工作与人才培养和职业规划相结合。一个学习型、复合型的团队，相信会为世博馆的发展注入活力。

Practice and Principles in Collectibles Acquisition during World Expo

Lorelei Liu, Director of World Expo Museum

I: Abstract

With the aim to pass on Expo legacy, preserve Expo essence and sustain Expo effect, World Expo Museum has been dedicated to collecting the exhibits, memorable articles displayed on Expos as well as the archives from the organizers and participants of World Expo. As a super international event, World Expo not only has to abide by the Convention Relating to International Exhibitions, but also observe the exhibit–related rules and regulations in the hosting countries in terms of finance, taxes, customs, donation, intellectual property right and exhibition management. Therefore, an overall consideration should be made in acquiring collectibles during Expos including the legal framework of the organizers, communication with the participants, restrictions on collection and Expo site management, and the characteristics in museum science. And the way of collecting is different from those by the museums in soliciting contributions from the public.

World Expo Museum has initiated two extensive collection acquisitions in Expo 2010 Shanghai China and Expo 2012 Yeosu Korea respectively since September, 2010. By March, 2013, the participants and organizers of Expo Shanghai (from 219 countries and regions) had donated 27 253 pieces and those of Expo Yeosu (from 44 countries and regions) contributed 706 pieces. Based on the collecting during these two World Expos (2010 and 2012), and the positioning and form as organizer and participant respectively by World Expo Museum, this paper aims to analyze the laws and principles in the targets, standards, regulations, management, operation and academic studies in our work, reveal the unique characteristics in acquiring collectibles during World Expo, and tentatively put forward innovative collecting models for museums.

II: Table of Contents

目录
Contents

DE 片区藏品精选

城市最佳实践区藏品精选

省区市联合馆藏品精选

上海世博会博物馆藏品捐赠

Contents
目录

Collection from Zone B

Collection from Zone C

Collection from Zone D&E

Collection from UBPA

Collection from Chinese Provinces Joint Pavilion

中国 2010 年上海世界博览会概况
Expo 2010 Shanghai China

主　　　题：城市，让生活更美好

类　　　别：注册类世界博览会

园　　　区：上海市中心黄浦江两岸，从南浦大桥到卢浦大桥以西的滨江地区

园 区 规 模：5.23 平方公里

运 营 时 间：2010 年 5 月 1 日至 2010 年 10 月 31 日

总参观人数：7 308 万人次

参展者数量：246 个国家和国际组织，包括 190 个国家和 56 个国际组织；80 个经典案例
　　　　　　组成展示世界城市发展的城市最佳实践区；25 个企业共建成 18 个企业馆。

中国 2010 年上海世博会以"城市，让生活更美好"为主题，来自全球的参展方共同围绕这一主题，充分展示城市文明成果、交流城市发展经验、传播先进城市理念，从而为新世纪人类的居住、生活和工作探索崭新的模式，为生态和谐社会的缔造和人类的可持续发展提供生动的例证。

在世博园区里，各参展方根据自身对城市主题的不同理解，精心设计展馆、策划展示内容，每个展馆都具有与众不同的魅力。

上海世博会园区划分为 A、B、C、D、E 五个功能片区，其中 A、B、C 三个功能片区分布在浦东地区，D、E 两个功能片区分布在浦西地区。其中，A 片区主要布置部分亚洲国家馆等场馆，B 片区主要布置城市人馆、城市生命馆、城市地球馆以及部分亚洲国家馆、大洋洲国家馆、国际组织馆等场馆，C 片区主要布置欧洲、美洲、非洲国家馆等场馆，D 片区主要布置城市足迹馆和企业馆等场馆，E 片区主要布置城市未来馆、企业馆和城市最佳实践区等场馆。

Theme: Better City, Better Life

Type: Registered International Exhibition

Expo Site: Along both sides of Huangpu River in downtown Shanghai, from Nanpu Bridge to west of Lupu Bridge.

Enclosed Area: 5.28 square kilometers

Duration: May 1, 2010 to October 31, 2010

Total visitors: 73.08 million person-times

Number of participants: 246 official participants, including 190 countries and 56 international organizations; 80 classic cases of city development around the world exhibiting in Urban Best Practices Area(UBPA); 25 corporate participants in 18 corporate pavilions.

Under the theme of "Better City, Better Life", Expo 2010 Shanghai China has attracted participants all over the world. It fully reveals the urban civilization, exchanges experiences of urban development and propagates advanced urban ideas, and, therefore, explores brand-new models for mankind's residence, living and work in the new century, offering a vivid example for the creation of an ecological and harmonious society and for the sustainable development.

According to the different comprehension of the urban theme, each of the participants meticulously designs their exhibition space and makes out their exhibition contents with unique charm.

The Expo site of Expo 2010 Shanghai China is divided into five functional zones of A, B, C, D and E. Amongst, A, B and C zones are in Pudong area, while D and E zones are in Puxi area. Particularly, Zone A is mainly for pavilions of some Asian nations. Zone B is mainly for the Urbanian Pavilion, the Pavilion of City Being and the Pavilion of Urban Planet as well as pavilions of some Asian nations, pavilions of Oceanian nations, pavilions of international organizations. Zone C is mainly for pavilions of European, American and African nations. Zone D is mainly for the Pavilion of Footprint and pavilions of enterprises. Zone E is mainly for the Pavilion of Future, pavilions of enterprises and UBPA.

2010 年上海世博会
藏品精选
Collections from
Expo 2010 Shanghai China

中国 2010 年上海世博会中国馆设计手稿
Design Manuscript for the China Pavilion of Expo 2010

捐赠方 / 上海世博会中国馆
Donated by / China Pavilion of Expo 2010

中国馆建筑设计手稿
Design Manuscript for the China Pavilion

中国馆建筑造型源于中国古代礼器，斗拱结构层叠出挑，庄重雄伟。中国馆领衔设计者、中国工程院院士、华南理工大学建筑学院院长何镜堂认为中国馆凸显了中国特色和时代精神，寓意"天下粮仓，富庶百姓"。

Inspired by the sacrificial vessels in ancient China, the main architecture of the China Pavilion is designed in the form of traditional Dougong or brackets featuring layer upon layer between the top of a column and a crossbeam, standing out as a majestically impressive building. He Jingtang, leading designer of the China Pavilion, academician of the Chinese Academy of Engineering and Director of the School of Architecture of South China University of Technology, remarks that the China Pavilion highlights the unique Chinese characteristics and the spirit of the era, implying "ample barn and rich people".

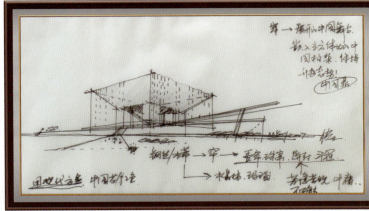

中国馆主题演绎
Interpretation of the Theme of the China Pavilion

中国馆的展示主题：城市发展中的中华智慧，旨在探索中国自身的城市化发展道路。

Theme of the China Pavilion: Wisdom of the Chinese people in Urban Development: to explore the approaches of urbanization in line with Chinese characteristics.

倒挂城市
City of Upside Down

城市的印象不光是高低错落的建筑群，更是生活其间的亿万城市人。

What is impressive about a city is not only the charming skyline of the buildings, but also the billions of dwellers living in it.

中国馆电影
Video in the China Pavilion

讲述改革开放三十多年来中国城市化进程中的经验及自强不息的精神、中国人民的建设热情和对于未来的期望。

A short video tells the unremitting efforts made by the Chinese people in urbanization over the past three decades of reform and opening up, their passion for building better cities and expectation for a bright future.

智慧的长河
River of Wisdom

现代科技再现了《清明上河图》的神韵，上千个人物角色均被赋予了生命，古代都市跃然眼前。

Thanks to state-of-art technologies, the well-known painting named "Riverside Scene at Qingming Festival" makes its presence in the China Pavilion in a vivid manner, with thousands of figures being endowed with energetic lives to illustrate the vigor of ancient Chinese cities.

同一屋檐下
Under the Same Roof

社区是城市的单元，人与人组成了城市活跃的细胞，在真实与虚拟、传统与现代之间，当代城市不能丢掉人际交往的传统。

A city consists of communities while individual people are cells of a city teaming with vitality. Sandwiched between reality and imagination, and tradition and modernity, people in modern cities can not afford to forsake interpersonal communication.

斗拱森林与折纸森林
Forest of Dougong and Folding-Paper

意象化的绿色植物建构出一个梦幻的绿色环境，其中还穿插新老城市人在同一屋檐下和谐相处的影像装置。

By means of imagery, green plants will feast your eyes with a wonderful world of green land, in which projectors are available to show the harmonious co-existence of the new-coming and old city dwellers living in the same place.

感悟之泉
Fountain of Illumination

"自强不息，厚德载物，师法自然，和而不同。"这是中国古人留给后人的"大智慧"，要应对城市化进程中出现的困难和挑战，需要充分发挥中华智慧的作用。

"Constant self-improving, social commitment, learning from the nature and harmonious co-existence" is the wisdom handed down from the ancient Chinese people to later generations. The Chinese wisdom shall be given full play in an effort to overcome difficulties and tackle challenges in the process of urbanization.

低碳行动
Low-Carbon Initiatives

聚集以低碳为核心元素的中国未来城市发展，展示中国人如何通过"师法自然的现代追求"来应对未来的城市化挑战，为实现全球可持续发展提供"中国式的回答"。

The exhibition focuses on the urban development of China in the future with low-carbon as its core. It shows how the Chinese people are inspired by the nature and propose their own solutions to address the challenges in urbanization and achieve global growth in a sustainable way.

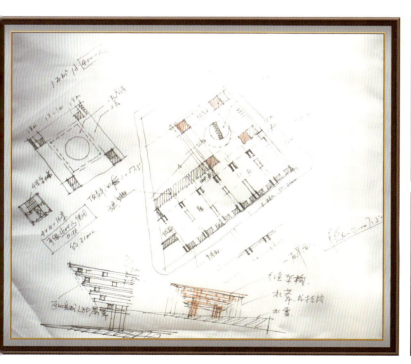

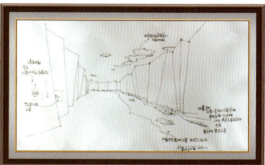

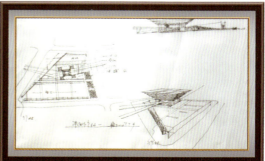

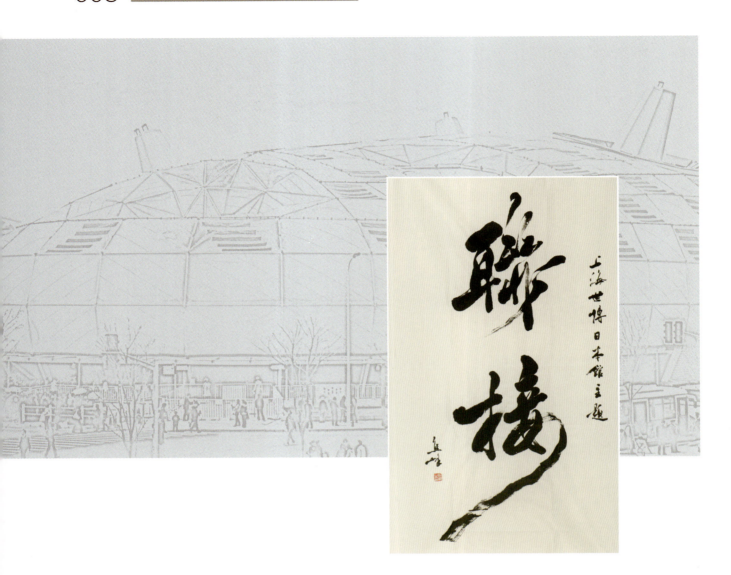

书法 "联接"
Handwriting "Linking (lian jie in Chinese)"

捐赠方 / 上海世博会日本馆
Donated by / Japan Pavilion of Expo 2010

2009 年 12 月 26 日，取名为 "紫蚕岛" 的日本馆举行了盛大的竣工仪式。在仪式上，旅日书法家熊峰现场挥毫书写了日本馆的主题关键词 "联接" 二字，希望人们超越国境与文化的不同，建立起人与人、人与自然之间更加和谐的关系。

At the completion ceremony of the Japan Pavilion on December 26, 2009, Xiong Feng, calligrapher from Japan, wrote two Chinese characters "lian jie" as the key words for the theme of the Japan Pavilion, expressing the wish that the bond between person and person and that between the human beings and nature become stronger despite diversities of cultures and separation of national boundaries.

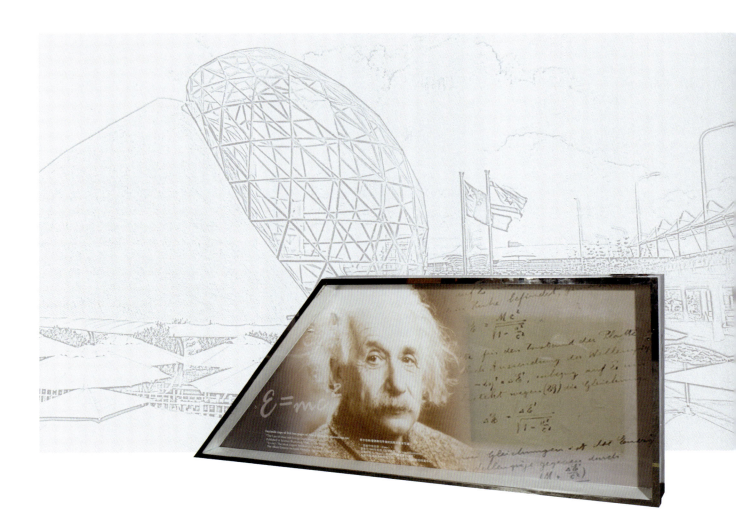

爱因斯坦相对论手稿（高仿品）
Einstein's Manuscript of "Theory of Relativity" (replica)

捐赠方 / 上海世博会以色列馆
Donated by / Israel Pavilion of Expo 2010

在以色列馆，最引人瞩目的展品莫过于爱因斯坦相对论手稿。相对论是关于时空和引力的基本理论，主要由爱因斯坦创立，分为狭义相对论和广义相对论。相对论颠覆了人类对宇宙和自然的常识性观念。

据以色列馆长施泰尼茨介绍，爱因斯坦生前曾将自己的一批重要手稿捐赠给希伯来大学，其中就包括这份文本，包含其亲手书写的著名相对论公式：$E=MC^2$。手稿在上海世博会上展出，得到了希伯来大学校方的支持，昭显了中以两国深厚的友谊。

The Israel Pavilion showcases a precious manuscript with the well-known formula of Relativity $E=MC^2$ written by Einstein, a world-famous scientist. The exhibition of the manuscript is made possible thanks to the support from the Hebrew University of Jerusalem, which embodies the profound friendship between China and Israel.

"和平之火"圣火传递灯及佛牌
"Fire of Peace" Holy Flame Lamp and Amulet

捐赠方 / 上海世博会尼泊尔国家馆日代表团
Donated by / Delegate of the National Pavilion Day of Nepal

"和平之火"取自佛教创始人释迦牟尼的诞生地——尼泊尔南部城市蓝毗尼。2010 年 8 月 18 日，由数百位高僧采集圣火火种放入传递灯并护送往上海世博会。

2010 年 9 月 3 日上海世博会尼泊尔国家馆日仪式上，尼泊尔国家馆日代表团向上海世博会组织方赠送该灯。尼泊尔副总理表示：采集圣火是尼泊尔国家历史上的一件大事。把圣火从蓝毗尼传到中国，表示中尼两国人民的友谊世代相传，同时也表示佛的智慧光明照耀尼泊尔、照耀中国、照耀世界。

On August 18, 2010, the holy flame was ignited by hundreds of eminent monks at the flame altar of Lumbini and then the holy flame lamp was escorted to the site of Expo 2010 Shanghai China. The delegate of the National Pavilion Day of Nepal gave the lamp to the organizing committee of Expo 2010 Shanghai China as a gift at the celebration ceremony of the National Pavilion Day of Nepal on September 3, 2010. The relaying of the holy flame from Lumbini to China not only represents the profound friendship from generation to generation between the people of Nepal and the people of China, but also sheds light on that the wisdom of Buddhist shines in Nepal, China and even the whole world.

海百合化石
Fossil of Crinoids

捐赠方 / 上海世博会东帝汶馆
Donated by / Timor-Leste Pavilion of Expo 2010

东帝汶馆远古海百合化石，生成于远古海底，有 2.5 亿年历史，具有较高的科研和考古价值。海百合对生存环境要求极其苛刻。

With a long history of more than 250 million years, the fossil of crinoids from Timor-Leste was formed in the sea since the remote antiquity. Crinoids have strict requirements in terms of the living conditions. It can serve as a reference of high value for scientific research and archaeological study.

"孟加拉民族战争" 纪念挂毯
Tapestry for Commemorating the "National War of Bangladesh"

捐赠方 / 上海世博会孟加拉国馆
Donated by / Bangladesh Pavilion of Expo 2010

上海世博会孟加拉国馆展示的挂毯，图案为该国民族战争的景象，表现了孟加拉国人民解放的历史。

Exhibited in the Bangladesh Pavilion, the tapestry has a pattern to show the national war of Bangladesh, reflecting the history of how the Bangladeshi was liberated.

智慧锁——车上的蒙古包
Wisdom Lock-Yurt on the Wheel

捐赠方 / 上海世博会蒙古馆
Donated by / Mongolia Pavilion of Expo 2010

蒙古是游牧民族国家，牧民需要根据四季的变换迁徙而居，于是就有了这种智慧锁——蒙古包。蒙古最杰出的拼搭设计师 Zandraa Tumen-Ulzii 设计的这件"智慧锁——车上的蒙古包"，由 2 万余片木块构成，在蒙古馆内由工匠 Muakh-Itgelt Tumen-Ulzii 耗时 3 天才将其拼搭完成。

As nomads, the herdsmen of Mongolia migrate in different seasons around the year, which is why the yurt on the wheel, wisdom lock, is born. Comprised over 20 thousand pieces of wood, the "wisdom lock-yurt on the wheel" took three days to complete.

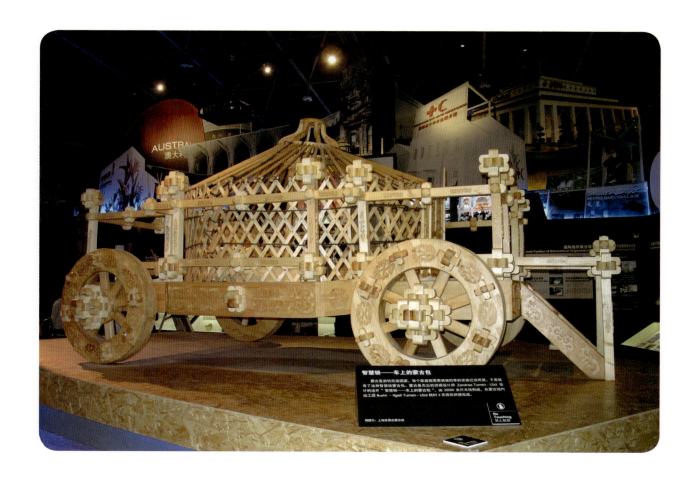

双刃弯刀
Jambiya

捐赠方 / 上海世博会也门馆
Donated by / Yemen Pavilion of Expo 2010

双刃弯刀的阿拉伯名为 Jambiya，意为"弧度特别的刀刃"。短刀通常被系在腰间，其价值取决于刀柄的工艺。在阿拉伯社会中，短刀象征着佩带者的地位和权力。

Jambiya is an Arabian word meaning "special-curved blade". A jambiya is usually tied against the waist with its value subject to the craftsmanship of hilt. In the Arabic society, it symbolizes the dignity and power of its wearer.

贝都因咖啡壶
Bedouin Coffee Pot

捐赠方 / 上海世博会约旦馆
Donated by / Jordan Pavilion of Expo 2010

贝都因人是阿拉伯人的一支，几千年来一直生活在地球上环境最恶劣的地区之一——阿拉伯沙漠中。为客人煮咖啡是贝都因传统接待礼仪中不可缺少的一项。主人会将咖啡豆焙制、冷却、研磨后用名为 DALLAH 的咖啡壶煮开，款待贵宾。

The Bedouin are a branch of Arabians who dwell in the Arabian Desert, one of the regions with the most adverse weather conditions on earth, for thousands of years. It is essential traditional hospitality etiquette of the Bedouin to make coffee for guests.

手工制木拼匣子
Handmade Mosaic-wood Box

捐赠方 / 上海世博会叙利亚馆
Donated by / Syria Pavilion of Expo 2010

叙利亚的手工艺品以独特的民族配色及图案、精细的手工艺闻名于世。手工木拼匣子是叙利亚手工艺品的代表，每个匣子的木盖上都镶有叙利亚名胜及风景画。

Handmade mosaic-wood box stands out among Syrian handicrafts, with a woody lid inlaid with Syrian scenic and landscape paintings.

花梨木佛雕屏风
Budda-carved Rosewood Screen

捐赠方 / 上海世博会老挝馆
Donated by / Laos Pavilion of Expo 2010

老挝盛产珍贵的花梨木木料，用其制作而成的雕塑、家具及工艺品受到世界各地的欢迎，且因数量日趋减少而愈发珍贵。这件巨幅花梨木雕刻以面容静谧微笑的佛像，展现了老挝花梨木的上好材质及独特雕刻风格。

Laos abounds with precious rosewood timbers whose preciousness keeps increasing as its quantity diminishes. With a Buddha wearing a serene smile being carved, this huge rosewood carving renders a delicate touch of Southeast Asia, demonstrating not only the top-ranking timber from Laos but also its unique carving style.

阿拉丁神灯
Lamp of Aladdin

捐赠方 / 上海世博会伊拉克馆
Donated by / Iraq Pavilion of Expo 2010

《一千零一夜》是著名的古代阿拉伯民间故事集，在中国一度被译为《天方夜谭》。"天方"是中国古代对阿拉伯地区的称呼，仅凭这名字，就足以把人带到神秘的异域世界中。

上海世博会伊拉克馆将《一千零一夜》作为展馆的主题，营造出书中奇幻美妙的阿拉伯宫殿。这个主题寓意着通过神灯能尽早实现伊拉克重建，希望让人们忘却伊拉克的战争和其所带来的创伤，带给人们对过去美好的回忆与对未来生活的憧憬。

Iraq Pavilion of Expo 2010 Shanghai China takes *The Thousand and One Nights* as its theme, implying the hope of Iraqis to reconstruct Iraq as soon as possible with the Lamp's power, eliminate the memory of wars and trauma inflicted upon Iraq and create sweet memory and bright prospect for the people.

孔雀乐琴
Myanmar Harp

捐赠方 / 上海世博会缅甸馆
Donated by / Myanmar Pavilion of Expo 2010

缅甸孔雀造型传统乐器，也被称之为"箜篌"，是十分古老的弹弦乐器。在古代除宫廷雅乐使用外，在民间也广泛流传。14 世纪后期，此乐器不再流行，并逐渐消失，人们只能在以前的壁画和浮雕上看到一些箜篌的图样。

Myanmar harp, also known as "Konghou", is an ancient plucked string instrument shaped in peacock. Since the late fourteenth century, it started to be out of mode and fall into total oblivion.

阿曼馆油画
Oil Paintings in Oman Pavilion

捐赠方 / 阿曼苏丹王国政府
Donated by / Government of the Sultanate of Oman

上海世博会阿曼馆内展示的油画，由阿曼艺术家为上海世博会主题"城市，让生活更美好"特别创作。

The oil paintings exhibited in Oman Pavilion of Expo 2010 Shanghai China are specially created by famous Oman artists contributing to the theme of Expo 2010 "Better City, Better Life".

猎鹰雕塑
Falcon Sculpture

捐赠方 / 上海世博会阿联酋馆
Donated by / UAE Pavilion of Expo 2010

阿联酋馆展示了纹样各异的猎鹰雕塑。

沙漠中的阿拉伯部落用猎鹰进行捕猎的历史可以追溯到 2 000 多年前，因为它出众的捕猎技巧，使得当地人能够在沙漠中极其单调的食物链中生存下来，因此阿拉伯人称它为"众鸟之王"。传说中沙漠王子的三件宝物就是：腰刀、骆驼和飞鹰。因此，猎鹰在阿拉伯国家，尤其是阿联酋，被认为是权利、财富和地位的象征。

Falcon sculptures with various patterns are exhibited outside UAE Pavilion. Dating back to more than 2 000 years ago, falcons have been used by Arabian tribes in the desert to hunt. In some countries (particularly UAE), falcons are regarded as the symbol of power, wealth and nobility. It is said that broadsword, camel and falcon are the three treasures of Desert Prince.

龙头石雕
Dragon Head Sculpture

捐赠方 / 上海世博会越南馆
Donated by / Vietnam Pavilion of Expo 2010

越南首都河内在历史上又名升龙。2010 年是越南首都河内建城一千年，所以此次参展上海世博会，越南将自己的参展主题定为"升龙——河内一千年"。

龙头石雕展现了越南古代历史及民族文化，体现出越南与我国自古以来紧密的文化交流与源远流长的邦交友谊。

Hanoi, the capital of Vietnam, is also known as Thang Long in history. In 2010 when Hanoi celebrated its 1000th anniversary since foundation, Vietnam chose" 1000-year-long History of Hanoi" as its theme to participate in Expo 2010. The dragon head sculpture represents the long-standing cultural communication between Vietnam and China and their well-established diplomatic relation.

"金兰之交"铜钱树
Tree of Close Friendship Made of Copper Coin

捐赠方 / 大韩贸易投资振兴公社
    上海世博会韩国馆
Donated by / Korea Trade-Investment Promotion Agency
    Republic of Korea Pavilion of Expo 2010

铜钱树雕塑由中央美术学院城市设计学院副院长王中教授与韩国著名雕塑家成熏东合作打造。

作品以中国成语"金兰之交"为主题,利用中韩两国历史上流传下来的铜钱与代表历经岁月沧桑的树木为元素,表现两国文化的交融。树枝上挂有 200 个代表果实的韩中传统古钟,随着内置风动装置发出悦耳的声响,寓意中韩两国情若金兰,友谊之树硕果累累。

Themed with a Chinese idiom describing close friendship, this copper coin tree combines two elements: copper coins handed down through the history of China and Republic of Korea, and trees representing weathered years. It embodies the communication between two countries, implying the close friendship shared between Republic of Korea and China and its great benefits for both.

朝鲜馆雕塑
Sculpture in Democratic People's Republic of Korea Pavilion

捐赠方 / 上海世博会朝鲜馆
Donated by / Democratic People's Republic of Korea Pavilion of Expo 2010

上海世博会朝鲜馆展馆中央的雕塑，五个男孩手牵手围成一圈，中间的孩子正在放飞白鸽。雕塑表达了朝鲜人民向往和平的心愿。

The sculpture in the center of Democratic People's Republic of Korea Pavilion of Expo 2010 consists of five boy figurines holding hands in a circle and one child in the center releasing a white dove, expressing the craving for peace.

阿希雷姆国王石棺（高仿品）
Sarcophagus of King Ahiram (replica)

捐赠方 / 上海世博会黎巴嫩馆
Donated by / Lebanon Pavilion of Expo 2010

放置在黎巴嫩馆入口处的阿希雷姆国王石棺在昏黄的灯光下显得庄重而神秘，引得游客纷纷驻足。该石棺虽然是一件复制品，但却也是由 8 名黎巴嫩雕塑家耗时 4 个月精心打造而成的，力求最大程度地复制。棺木上的腓尼基文铭文，是人类现存最早的字母文本，距今已有 3 000 年历史。

腓尼基字母是希伯来字母、阿拉伯字母、希腊字母和拉丁字母的"祖先"。而阿希雷姆国王石棺的出土证明了腓尼基文字是世界上现存最早的拼音文字，并证明了黎巴嫩是字母文字的摇篮。在 2010 年上海世博会上，石棺的展示揭开了最古老人类文明的面纱一角。

2005 年，德国约翰内斯·古滕贝格大学教授莱因哈德·莱曼最终破译了石棺上这段铭文的内容：

"此棺椁由比布鲁斯国王阿希雷姆为父亲老阿希雷姆升入'永恒之家'而造。如果有国王、统治者或军队首领胆敢踏入比布鲁斯，并打开这个石棺，那么他的权杖将会粉碎，他的王位将被颠覆，他将走向地狱，比布鲁斯将不再和平。"

The sarcophagus is forged by 8 sculptors from Lebanon in 4 months in an effort to replicate the original to the greatest extent. With a history for 3 000 years, the Phoenician epigraph carved in it is the earliest alphabetic text discovered by the human beings.

By unearthing the sarcophagus of King Ahiram, it is proved that Phoenician is the earliest alphabetic script existing in the world and that Lebanon is the cradle for alphabetic scripts. At Expo 2010, the sarcophagus was exhibited to give a glimpse of the most ancient human civilization.

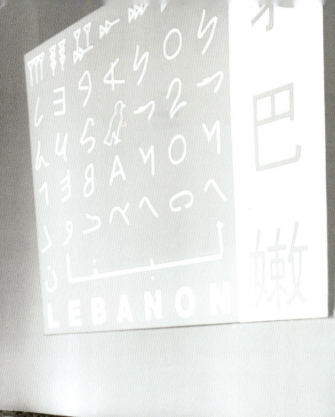

LEBANON
黎巴嫩

担担鼓
Tam Tam Drum

捐赠方 / 上海世博会瓦努阿图馆
Donated by / Vanuatu Pavilion of Expo 2010

太平洋岛国木雕
Wood Carvings from Pacific Islands

捐赠方 / 上海世博会巴布亚新几内亚馆
Donated by / Papua New Guinea Pavilion of Expo 2010

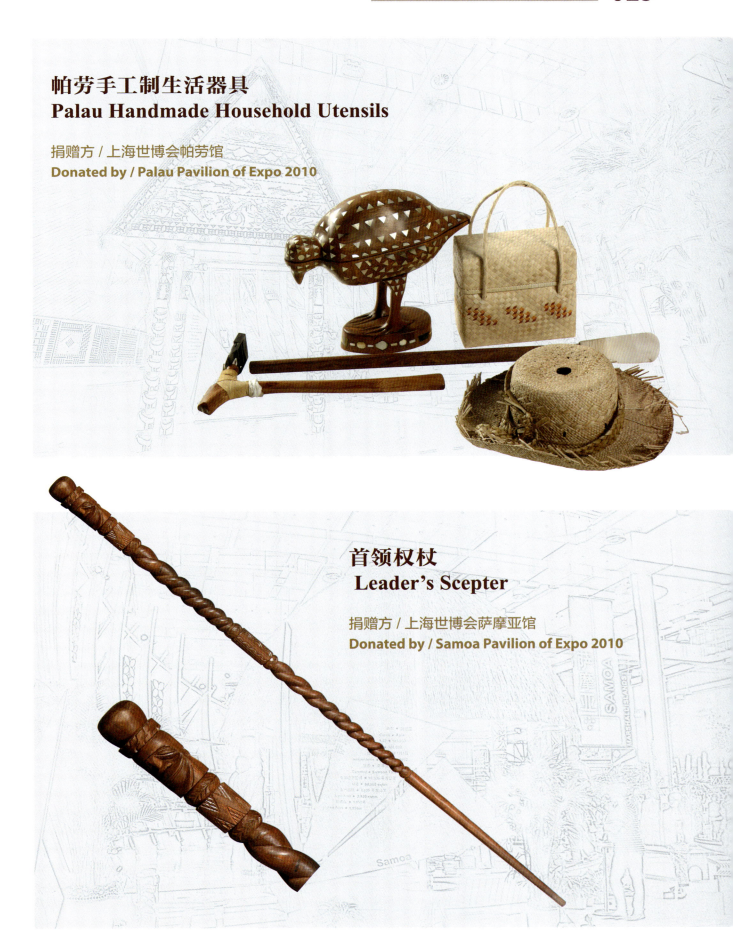

帕劳手工制生活器具
Palau Handmade Household Utensils

捐赠方 / 上海世博会帕劳馆
Donated by / Palau Pavilion of Expo 2010

首领权杖
Leader's Scepter

捐赠方 / 上海世博会萨摩亚馆
Donated by / Samoa Pavilion of Expo 2010

斐济独木舟
Fijian Canoe

捐赠方 / 上海世博会斐济馆
Donated by / Fiji Pavilion of Expo 2010

在斐济，独木舟是一种重要的雕刻艺术品。在传统中，它被用作交通工具、典礼展示品甚至战斗装备。斐济最令人印象深刻的独木舟叫"DRUA"，它是大洋洲工艺品中最为精美的一种。

一艘真实的 DRUA 独木舟能够搭载 150 人。一艘独木舟的建成通常需要 6 至 7 年时间，其长度大约为 100 至 118 英尺，船舷的高度大约为 60 至 70 英尺。

In Fiji which is an island country, canoe is the primary vehicle. The most impressive canoe in Fiji is called "DRUA", which usually can carry 150 people and takes 6-7 years to construct.

木质人像雕塑
Wood Portrait Sculpture

捐赠方 / 上海世博会库克群岛馆
Donated by / Cook Islands Pavilion of Expo 2010

所罗门群岛神像
DIRKA DIGURE from Solomon Islands

捐赠方 / 上海世博会所罗门群岛馆
Donated by / Solomon Islands Pavilion of Expo 2010

草编工艺品
Straw Crafts

捐赠方 / 上海世博会图瓦卢馆
Donated by / Tuvalu Pavilion of Expo 2010

马绍尔群岛独木舟
Canoe from Marshall Islands

捐赠方 / 上海世博会马绍尔群岛馆
Donated by / Marshall Islands Pavilion of Expo 2010

庆典鼓
Celebration Drum

捐赠方 / 上海世博会太平洋联合馆
Donated by / Pacific Joint Pavilion of Expo 2010

木鼓由法属波利尼西亚岛国原著民手工雕刻而成。鼓的四角分别雕刻有四个小人，托举着刻有神明图腾的鼓身，雕刻精美，构思巧妙。庆典鼓用于祭祀或庆典时舞蹈的伴奏。庆典鼓是波利尼西亚民俗民情的一个载体。

This wooden drum is carved by the aborigines living on French Polynesia. The drum is sophisticatedly structured and exquisitely carved, four corners of which are carved as four little figurines holding the drum body carved with god totem. Celebration drum is used as an accompaniment instrument to dances at rituals or celebrations.

大溪地图腾木柱
Tahitian Totem Pole

捐赠方 / 上海世博会太平洋联合馆
Donated by / Pacific Joint Pavilion of Expo 2010

木柱上雕刻有大溪地地域色彩的图腾，取材于当地的热带树木，雕刻着太平洋岛屿人们所崇拜事物的写意形象，展现了热带岛屿上原住民的精神崇拜和地域风俗。

The wooden pole is made of local tropical wood and carved with totems characteristic of Tahitian features and impressionistic images of the objects worshiped by Pacific islanders, demonstrating the spiritual worship and conventions of the aborigines on tropical islands.

柬埔寨吴哥窟石雕
Stone Carvings from Angkor Wat of Cambodia

捐赠方 / 上海世博会柬埔寨馆
Donated by / Cambodia Pavilion of Expo 2010

象头神迦尼萨石雕
Elephant God Ganesha

象头神迦尼萨是印度教的智慧之神，外形为断去一边象牙的象头人身，并长有四只手臂。因为迦尼萨是创生和破除障碍之神，被视为帮助信众接近其他神祇的使者神，能为世人带来成功和幸福。

Ganesha is the god of wisdom in Hinduism, being incarnated as an elephant-headed human with one broken tusk and four arms. As the god of creation and with the power to strike and repel obstacles, Ganesha is also regarded as the god of messenger helping believers approach other gods and bringing about success and happiness.

阁耶跋摩七世国王头像石雕
Head Sculpture of King Jayavarman VII

柬埔寨馆阁耶跋摩七世国王头像石雕，采用在柬埔寨政府批准下才可使用的吴哥窟特有石料雕刻而成。

The stone sculpture of King Jayavarman VII in Cambodia Pavilion is carved out of a special stone from Angkor Wat which can only be used with the approval of Cambodian government.

天女之舞浮雕
Apsara Relief

柬埔寨馆天女之舞浮雕，以细腻的雕刻手法再现了柬埔寨婀娜多姿的传统舞蹈，是吴哥窟石雕的经典纹样。

The Apsara Relief in Cambodia Palivion reproduces the magnificent scenario of Cambodian traditional dances in exquisite carvings, representing the classic stone carving pattern of Angkor Wat.

泰国门神"因陀罗耆特"和"蓝昙"
Thailand Door God "Indrajit" & "Luntun"

捐赠方 / 泰国社会发展和人类保障部
Donated by / Ministry of Social Development and Human
Security, Thailand

上海世博会泰国馆门口左右分别 "站立"着两位巨大的门神，分别是泰国传统门神 "因陀罗耆特"和中国元素的门神 "蓝昙"。泰国馆吉祥物 "小阿泰"的形象就来源于 "因陀罗耆特"。

在泰国，门神都面朝内站立在门外。而在中国，门神都被画成年画，面朝外张贴在门上。上海世博会泰国馆的两尊泰国门神都面朝外站立，欢迎每一位来客，这种方式是中泰两国风俗的融合，也是两国友好的象征。

Thailand traditional door god Indrajit and the door god Luntun with Chinese elements stand respectively on the right and left of the gate to Thailand Pavilion of Expo 2010 Shanghai China. In Thailand, door gods stand outside of doors facing inwards, while New Year pictures depicting door gods in China are posted on doors facing outwards. Both of the Thailand door gods in Thailand Pavilion stand facing outwards, which not only shows the integration of two countries' customs but also represents the friendly relationship between the two countries.

守护神"凯提亚奇"面具
Spiritual Guardian Mask Kaitiaki

捐赠方 / 上海世博会新西兰馆
Donated by / New Zealand Pavilion of Expo 2010

在新西兰，有一句话自古流传："人世更替，而大地永存。""凯提亚奇"在新西兰毛利文化中有着天空、海洋和大地的看护者、守护者及管理者的含义。

"凯提亚奇"传达着新西兰的一个核心理念——"凯提亚奇唐加"，即毛利文化中护卫环境的理念，这一思想体系充分阐述了为当今人类及子孙后代的共同利益而保护自然资源的重要性，呼吁人们在城市化进程中能够更注重大地、环境的保护，使我们的家园更美好。

Kaitiaki conveys one of the New Zealand's core concepts Kaitiakitanga. This is a concept about environment protection in Maori culture, explaining the importance of resource protection for the common benefits of the human beings and the later generations.

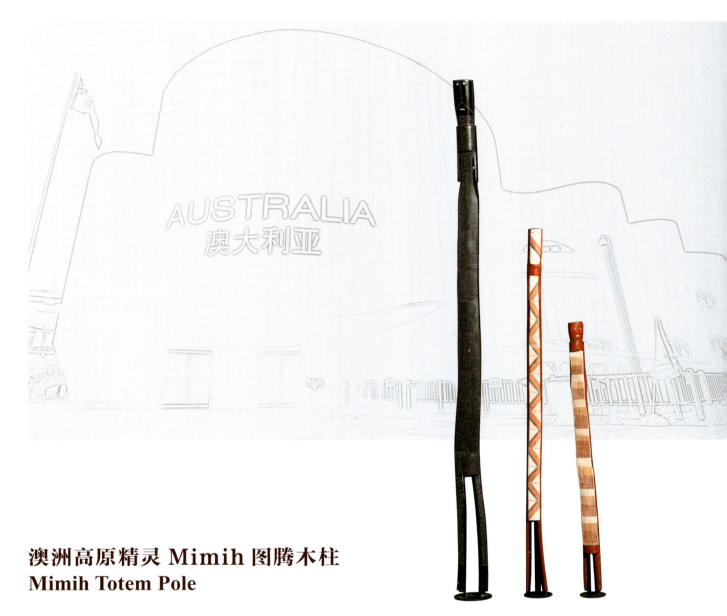

澳洲高原精灵 Mimih 图腾木柱
Mimih Totem Pole

捐赠方 / 上海世博会澳大利亚馆
Donated by / Australia Pavilion of Expo 2010

澳大利亚馆开篇之旅中的展示内容为"基岩"。澳大利亚北领地马宁里达镇文化与艺术中心的艺术设计师们用 30 根木头浇铸树脂及钢料雕成 Mimih 柱，代表了来自澳大利亚阿纳姆地高原穴居精灵 Mimi。

Mimi 的名字可能来源于珍珠鸟。这种小精灵被描述为具有极单薄和细长的身体，瘦小到会被风吹跑。他们通常生活在岩石裂缝中。据说，是他们教澳大利亚的原住民如何狩猎和使用火。他们就像人类，但生活在一个不同的维度。阿纳姆地高原的山岩上有描绘他们形象的古老壁画。

Mimih 体现了人类与大地之间的密切关系，这是澳大利亚历史与文化中亘古不变的主题，也是澳大利亚馆对本届世博会主题的一种呼应。

The art designers from Maningrida Arts & Culture Center, Northern Territory, Australia use 30 timbers cast with resin and steel to carve the Mimih pole, representing "Mimi", the cave fairy living on Australian Arnhem Land Plateau.

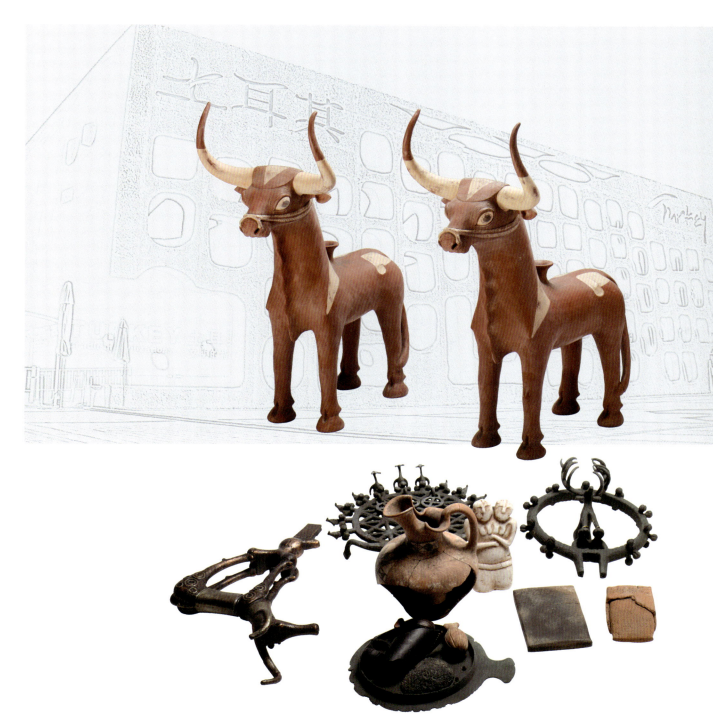

土耳其陶瓷雕塑及铁质装饰品
Turkish Ceramic Sculptures and Iron Decorations

捐赠方 / 上海世博会土耳其馆
Donated by / Turkey Pavilion of Expo 2010

土耳其馆的陶瓷制牛雕塑、陶罐、人像以及铁质装饰品。

Ceramic bull sculptures, clay pots, statues and iron decorations in Turkey Pavilion.

"撒尿小童"雕像（复制品）
Manneken-Pis Statute (replica)

捐赠方 / 上海世博会比利时馆
Donated by / Belgium-EU Pavilion of Expo 2010

撒尿小童铜像及喷水池是布鲁塞尔的城市标志。这尊青铜小童雕像原作建于 1619 年，高约 53 厘米，由比利时雕刻家杰罗姆·杜奎斯诺伊所打造。

1698 年，撒尿小童首次穿上衣服。此后，各国官员大使来比利时访问，都会特别做一套衣服送给他，于是这个"小男孩"拥有自己的专属衣柜，存放有七百多件世界各国赠送的衣服。目前衣服收藏皆展出于市区博物馆。中国 2010 年上海世博会上，撒尿小童穿上了中国传统服饰——"唐装"，受到参观者的热烈欢迎。

Created by Jerôme Duquesnoy, a Belgian sculptor, Manneken-Pis statute and fountain is the city logo of Brussels. At Expo 2010 Shanghai China, Manneken-Pis in Chinese traditional clothes Tang suits becomes a favorite of visitors.

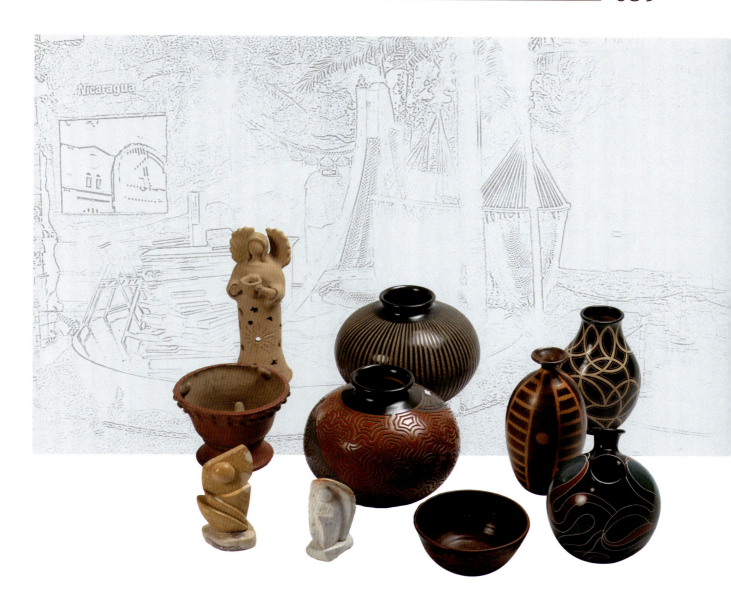

陶瓷工艺品
Ceramic Art Works

捐赠方 / 上海世博会尼加拉瓜馆
Donated by / Nicaragua Pavilion of Expo 2010

尼加拉瓜是"湖泊与火山之国"，陶器是该国代表性的手工艺品。这些陶器造型独特可爱，做工质朴，展示了尼加拉瓜热情大方、自然淳朴的民俗风貌。

Nicaragua is the country of lakes and volcanoes and ceramic is the representative artificial craft of this country. Unique in model and plain in craftsmanship, these ceramic crafts demonstrate the friendly, generous, natural and honest characteristics of Nicaragua folks.

"小美人鱼" 工艺品
"The Little Mermaid" Tableware

捐赠方 / 上海世博会丹麦馆
Donated by / Denmark Pavilion of Expo 2010

这件工艺品是根据"小美人鱼"雕像的外观制作而成的。

"小美人鱼"雕像是丹麦雕塑家爱德华·埃里克森根据安徒生童话《海的女儿》中女主人公的形象用青铜浇铸的，于1913年8月被安放在哥本哈根长堤公园海边的礁石上，多年来一直被视为丹麦的象征。

2009年3月12日，哥本哈根市议会通过投票同意让小美人鱼雕像进驻上海世博会丹麦馆，雕像于3月25日抵达上海世博园区。这是"小美人鱼"第一次走出丹麦国门。

Based on the fairy tale of the same name by Hans Christian Andersen, The Little Mermaid is a statue cast with copper. In August 1913, it was placed on a rock in the harbour off Langelinie promenade in Copenhagen. Since then, it is regarded as the symbol of Denmark.

手工编制装饰品
Hand Made Woven Decorations

捐赠方 / 上海世博会白俄罗斯馆
Donated by / Belarus Pavilion of Expo 2010

白俄罗斯的手工艺匠人使用简单草叶编制成花篮，逼真的形态、美妙的设计使装饰品如同鲜花般美丽灿烂。

Belarusian artisans use simple grass leaves to weave baskets, making splendid and lifelike decorations by neat design.

许愿石（复制品）
Wish Stone (replica)

捐赠方 / 上海世博会立陶宛馆
Donated by / Lithuania Pavilion of Expo 2010

世博会期间，一块神奇的许愿石被从立陶宛首都维尔纽斯城市广场上搬来，它不但见证了立陶宛国家的独立，还希望能够帮人们达成愿望。来到立陶宛馆的游客被邀请站在这块彩色地砖上，转动身体三圈，写下心愿并投入旁边的箱子，据说如此就可美梦成真。

The Wish Stone was originally placed on the city square in Vilnius, the capital of Lithuania. It is believed that one can realize his dream if he whirls around three times standing on this color tile, writes down his wish and tosses it into the adjacent box.

装饰锻造铁及钉珠装饰品
Ornamental Malleable Iron & Beaed Decoration

捐赠方 / 上海世博会海地馆
Donated by / Haiti Pavilion of Expo 2010

具有海地地理特征装饰锻造铁工艺品和手工制钉珠工艺品。

Malleable iron crafts with ornaments of Haitian geographic features and the hand-made beaed decorations.

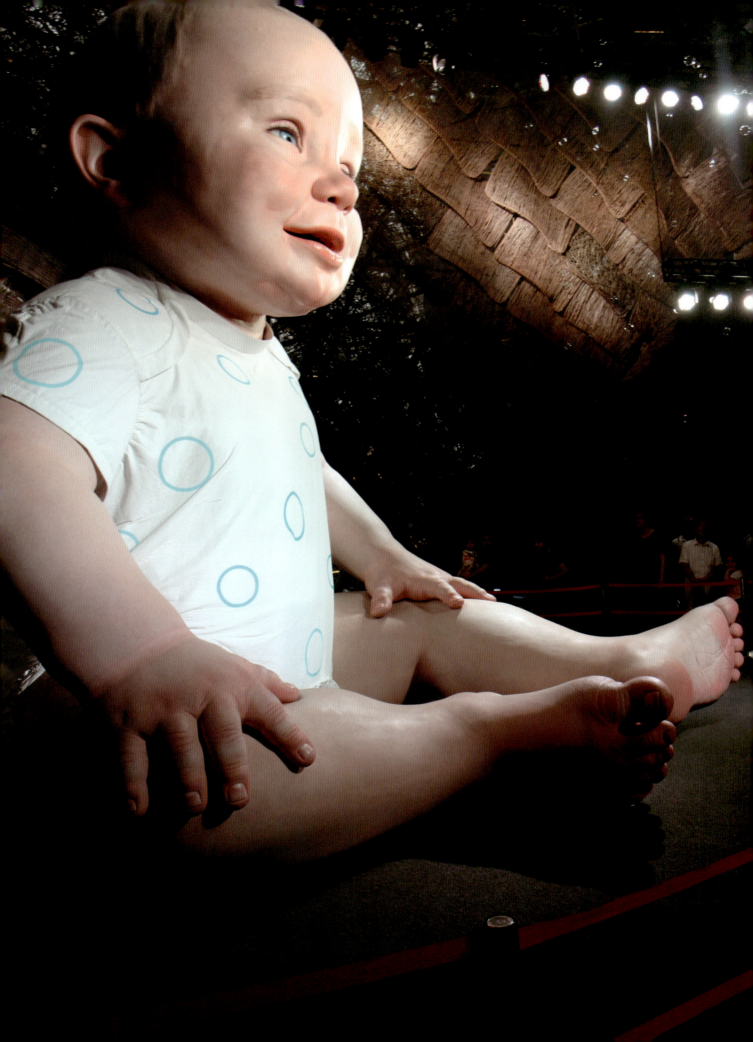

小米宝宝
Miguelin

捐赠方 / 西班牙国家国际展览署
Donated by / International Exhibition Commission of Spain

"小米宝宝"在上海世博会西班牙馆内展出，设计师为 Isabel Coixet。机器人娃娃"小米宝宝"，坐高达 6.5 米，由西班牙馆特意为参展上海世博会而制作，并由西班牙馆方赠予世博会博物馆。

2010 年 10 月 18 日，西班牙馆方向上海世博会博物馆捐赠"小米宝宝"，西班牙副首相、经济及税务部部长爱莲娜·赛尔加多与上海市政府副秘书长、上海世博局局长洪浩出席捐赠仪式并致辞。"小米宝宝"成为上海世博会博物馆首件获赠藏品。

在藤条建筑的围裹中，象征着城市文明如同摇篮孕育了人类生命。西班牙馆"小米宝宝"寓意着在未来的城市，每个孩子都能得到义务教育，每位公民都能享受医疗服务。

"Miguelin" by Isabel Coixet was exhibited in Spain Pavilion of Expo 2010 Shanghai China. The robot baby "Miguelin" with a sitting height of 6.5m was made by Spain Pavilion specially for exhibition of Expo 2010 and was donated by Spain Pavilion to World Exposition Museum.

On October 18, 2010, the Spain Pavilion presented "Baby Miguelin" to the Shanghai World Expo Museum. Elena Salgado, the then Deputy Prime Minister of Spain and Minister of Economy and Finance, and Hong Hao, Deputy Secretary-General of the Shanghai Municipal People's Government and Director of the Bureau of Shanghai World Expo Coordination attended and addressed at the donation ceremony. "Baby Miguelin" became the first collection received by the Shanghai World Expo Museum.

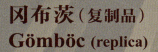

冈布茨（复制品）
Gömböc (replica)

捐赠方 / 匈牙利公共管理和司法部
Donated by / Ministry of Public Administration and Justice, Hungary

上海世博会匈牙利馆内展示的"冈布茨"是一种特殊的三维凸均匀体，诞生于 2006 年，是由匈牙利布达佩斯科技经济大学力学材料结构系耗费 10 年创造的新物理形态——世界上首个只有一个稳定平衡点和一个非稳定平衡点、且两个点在同一平面上的均质体。其最大特征是无论以何种角度放置在水平面上，冈布茨都可以自行回到稳定点。

冈布茨象征了和谐与平衡，也代表着匈牙利总是能从挫折中"重新站立起来"。同时，冈布茨也同东方文化中"阴阳"理论有千丝万缕的联系——两者都代表着对和谐与平衡的终极追求，这也是匈牙利人民在城市化发展道路上一直遵循的理念。

Gömböc is created by the Department of Mechanics, Materials and Structures at Budapest University of Technology and Economics in Hungary. Its most striking characteristic is that it can automatically return to a stable point whatever angle it is placed on the flat plane in. Gömböc represents Hungary who can always "revive" from setbacks and takes harmony and balance as its ultimate pursuit. This also conforms to the philosophies followed by Hungarians in urbanization development.

芬兰馆参展上海世博会纪念银币
Silver Memorial Coins Exhibited by Finland Pavilion of Expo 2010

捐赠方 / 上海世博会芬兰馆
Donated by / Finland Pavilion of Expo 2010

纪念币的图案由中央美术学院教授肖勇为芬兰特别设计。肖勇 20 世纪 90 年代曾留学于芬兰，任国际平面设计联合会副会长，为 2008 年北京奥运会奖牌的主创设计师。

纪念币的一面以芬兰馆独特的"冰壶"建筑为元素，用圆形体现祥和的意境。另一面汲取芬兰自然之美妙，意象地采用年轮和水波表达芬兰的创新与自然的和谐。纪念币的包装盒选取芬兰特有的桦木，用圆形和富有亲和力的回转结构，体现自然的轮回及与汉字"合"（和谐）的美妙。

The memorial coin incorporates the unique Kirnu on one side and the growth rings and ripples to show innovation and harmony with nature on the other side. The packing box of memorial coins is made of birch unique to Finland, revealing the recycle of nature and the marvel of Chinese character "合".

古希腊木船模型
Model of Ancient Greek Wooden Boat

捐赠方 / 希腊外贸协会
Donated by / HEPO S.A.

上海世博会希腊馆展厅中展示了一艘尚未完工的木船的复制品。尚未完工的木船停泊在希腊爱琴海的哈尼亚港中。展品与场景表现了希腊古代航海传统，以及该国在当今航海业的领先地位。大海在古希腊城市的发展过程中一直发挥着重要的作用。

Greek Pavilion of Expo 2010 Shanghai China exhibited a replica of an unfinished wooden boat berthing in Aegean Sea in Greece. The exhibition and scenario manifests the leading role of Greece in ancient navigation traditions and current navigation industry.

阿尔及利亚参展上海世博会纪念牌及邮册
Memorial Plate and Album Exhibited by Algeria Pavilion of Expo 2010

捐赠方 / 上海世博会阿尔及利亚馆
Donated by / Algeria Pavilion of Expo 2010

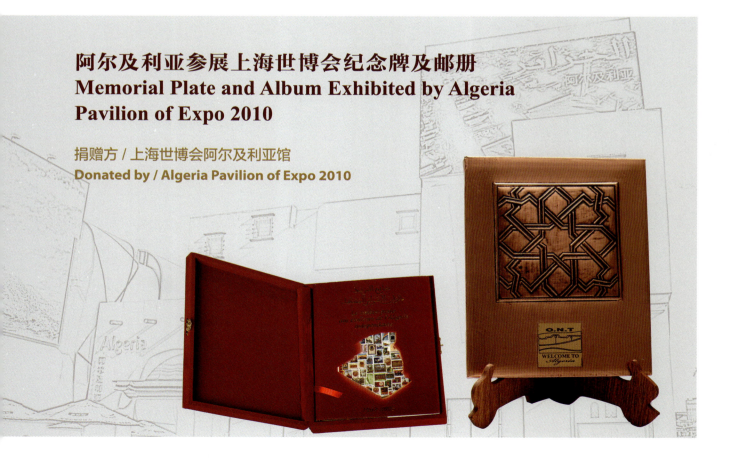

银质花朵
Silver Flower

捐赠方 / 上海世博会阿根廷馆
Donated by / Argentina Pavilion of Expo 2010

阿根廷在西班牙语中就是"银"的意思。银色花朵由阿根廷银器大师马赛罗·托雷多设计，象征国家之间的纯洁友谊。

Argentina means "silver" in Spanish. Silver Flower is designed by the silversmith Marcelo Toledo from Argentina, representing the pure friendship between two countries.

亚克力种子
The Acrylic Seeds

捐赠方 / 上海世博会英国馆
Donated by / UK Pavilion of Expo 2010

英国馆的设计是一个没有屋顶的开放式城市公园，其核心"种子圣殿"建筑外形由6万根内含各种植物种子的透明亚克力杆组成。这些种子由中国昆明种子植物研究所、英国皇家植物园与基尤千年种子银行共同提供。

"种子圣殿"的使命是为这个星球上高度复杂的植物生命体保存下活的档案，以防最坏的情况发生或入侵物种的破坏。"种子圣殿"代表了丰富的生物多样性并力求通过这种多样性为人类提供应变力、创造力和恢复力，意味着创新和探索的无限可能。

作为展示空间，"种子圣殿"为游客们提供了一个可以看到世界各地的野生植物的场所，一个使人沉思遐想的空间。

The core zone in UK Pavilion, known as the Seed Cathedral, is composed by 60 000 transparent acrylic rods housing various plant seeds. Those seeds were jointly offered by Kunming Institute of Botany from China, Royal Botanic Gardens and Kew Millennium Seed Bank in UK. The Seed Cathedral shows the rich biological diversity, creativity and infinite possibility.

自由女神像
The Statue of Liberty

捐赠方 / 上海世博会圣马力诺馆
Donated by / San Marino Pavilion of Expo 2010

这尊以一位年轻、勇敢的女子形象塑造的自由女神雕像原作于 1876 年的 9 月
30 日被公布于世，矗立在圣马力诺共和国首都议会大楼前的自由广场上。圣马
力诺是世界上历史最为悠久的共和国之一，而自由女神像被视为其几个世纪以
来独立和主权的象征。

上海世博会圣马力诺馆内的自由女神像雕像根据光学定位制作，与原雕塑完全
一致。

As one of the oldest republic countries in the world, San Marino has regarded
the Statue of Liberty as the symbol of independence and sovereignty for a
couple of centuries. In the San Marino Pavilion of Expo 2010 Shanghai stands
the identical replica of Statue of Liberty built by optical localization.

传统手工艺品
Traditional Crafts

捐赠方 / 上海世博会阿塞拜疆馆
Donated by / Azerbaijan Pavilion of Expo 2010

采用阿塞拜疆具有民族配色及传统手工艺制作的精美工艺品。

Exquisite crafts made in national colors and with traditional craftsmanship of Azerbaijan.

牛角酒杯
Ox Horn Cup

捐赠方 / 上海世博会格鲁吉亚馆
Donated by / Georgia Pavilion of Expo 2010

采用天然牛角打磨制成酒杯，镶嵌以银质装饰。牛角酒杯既是与美酒相配的珍贵酒杯，也是具有格鲁吉亚民族风格的工艺品。

The cup is made of natural ox horn by polishing and inlaid with silver decorations. It is not only a precious cup to match good wine and also a craft featuring the national style of Georgia.

科托尔的城门钥匙（复制品）
Kotor's Gate Key (replica)

捐赠方 / 上海世博会黑山馆
Donated by / Montenegro Pavilion of Expo 2010

城门钥匙在欧洲象征着对城市的绝对控制权。黑山馆将科托尔城门铜钥匙带到世博会，希望在它的引领下，来自世界各地的参观者将能开启黑山的古老文明智慧之门。

Montenegro Pavilion brought the copper gate key of Kotor to World Expo, wishing that visitors from all over the world may open the gate to the wisdom of ancient civilization of Montenegro with its guidance.

人形葡萄酒酒壶
Human-shaped wine pot

摩尔多瓦手工制酒器葡萄酒酒壶
Moldova Hand Made Wine Pots

捐赠方 / 上海世博会摩尔多瓦馆
Donated by / Moldova Pavilion of Expo 2010

摩尔多瓦的肥沃土地培育了珍贵的酿酒葡萄品种，泥土更可以制成善于保存红酒最佳口感的陶瓷酒壶。摩尔多瓦人民以其智慧将酒壶制作技艺精粹升华，造就了一件件艺术珍品。

The fertile soil of Moldova nourishes precious wine grapes and can be used to make ceramic wine pots helping preserve the best flavor of wine. The wisdom of the people of Moldova contributes to improve the wine pot craftsmanship greatly, making them fabulous arts.

葡萄形陶瓷酒壶
Grape-shaped wine pot

国徽浮雕葡萄酒酒壶
National emblem relief wine pot

黑陶酒罐
Black pottery wine jar

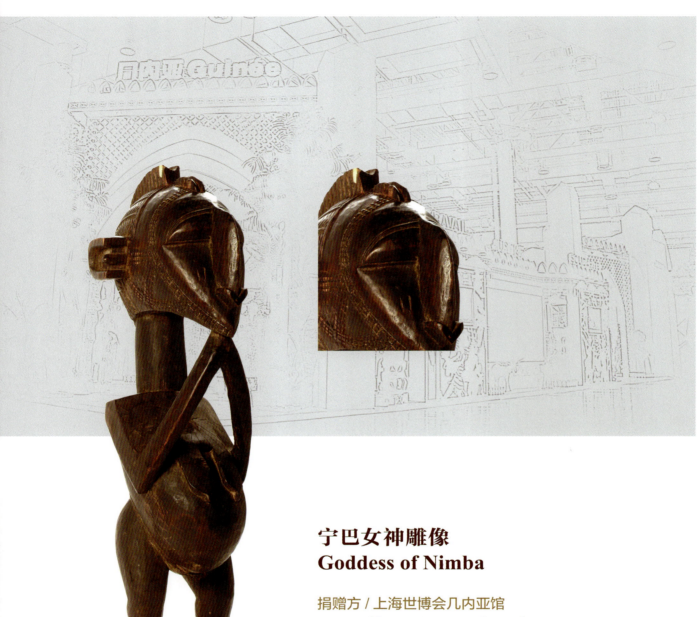

宁巴女神雕像
Goddess of Nimba

捐赠方 / 上海世博会几内亚馆
Donated by / Guinea Pavilion of Expo 2010

宁巴女神雕像采用珍贵的乌木雕刻，正面看是一个充满母爱的怀孕的女性，侧面看却像一只苍鹰。女神鲜明的女性特征既有母爱之情，也有祈求丰收之意，是非洲人祈求生育和丰收的神祇。

Carved out of ebony, the Goddess of Nimba looks like a pregnant woman exuding maternal love from the front side but like an eagle in profile. It is the goddess to whom Africans pray for fertility and harvest.

杰内大清真寺面具
Mask in the Great Mosque of Djenné

捐赠方 / 上海世博会几内亚比绍馆
Donated by / Guinea-Bissau Pavilion of Expo 2010

杰内大清真寺内独具非洲民族信仰象征的大型木质面具。

Large wooden mask with the unique symbol of African national belief in the Great Mosque of Djenné

马里手工制皮箱
Hand Made Leather Trunk from Mali

捐赠方 / 上海世博会马里馆
Donated by / Mali Pavilion of Expo 2010

采用整块上好皮革制作而成的皮箱是马里著名的特产，展现了非洲人民如何将智慧和精湛的手工艺融入生活中。

The leather trunk made of one-piece classy leather is the well-known specialty of Mali, showing how the Africans integrate wisdom and excellent craftsmanship into life.

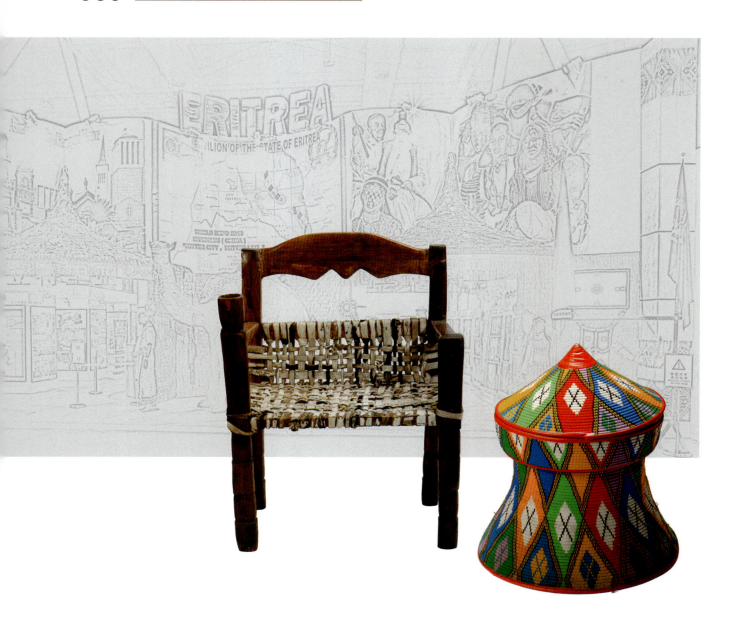

牛皮制餐椅及储物桌
Cow Leather Dining Chair and Storage Table

捐赠方 / 上海世博会厄立特里亚馆
Donated by / Eritrean Pavilion of Expo 2010

在厄立特里亚家庭中，许多家具都是用牛皮和木材制成的。当地人在吃饭时会坐在这种特别的餐椅上，一旁的扶手上有放置饮料的搁置设计。储物桌完全由手工编制而成，造型独特，色彩传统，用以储藏食物。

The Eritrean dining chair has a shelf on the armrest to place beverage. The storage table is completely hand made, featuring a unique shape and traditional colors.

中国 2010 年上海世博会徽标造型木雕
Wood Carved Logo of Expo 2010

捐赠方 / 上海世博会中非馆
Donated by / Central African Republic Pavilion of Expo 2010

木雕是中非馆为上海世博会特制。两种肤色的双手共同托举起中国 2010 年上海世博会的标志，寓意着中非人民对这一盛会的积极参与和衷心祝贺。

The wood carving is specially made by Central African Republic Pavilion of Expo 2010 Shanghai China. Two hands in two colors raise the logo of Expo 2010 Shanghai China, implying the positive participation in and hearted congratulations of Central Africans to this event.

陶瓷人偶
Ceramic Dolls

捐赠方 / 上海世博会贝宁馆
Donated by / Benin Pavilion of Expo 2010

色彩艳丽、造型各异、神态逼真的陶瓷人偶展现了贝宁人民生活的方方面面，表达了他们对生活的热爱。

The colorful, lifelike ceramic dolls with various shapes reveal every aspect of the daily life of Benin people and show their passion for life.

非洲科拉琴
Kora

捐赠方 / 上海世博会冈比亚馆
Donated by / Gambia Pavilion of Expo 2010

如果说非洲传统的打击乐带给人们的是奔放的热情，那么来自西非的科拉琴让人领略的就是非洲音乐的另一种特质——祥和。

科拉琴是一种流传于西非的 21 弦琴，演奏方法犹如弗拉明戈吉他般复杂多样。许多非洲民族的历史就是伴着科拉琴的旋律，一代一代传唱下来的。

Kora is a 21-string harp popular in West Africa, revealing the soft and emotional elements in African music. The history of many African tribes is passed down from generation to generation accompanied by Kora.

毛里求斯馆上海世博会特制蓝便士首日封
Twopenny Blue First Day Cover Specially Made by Mauritius Pavilion for Expo 2010

捐赠方 / 上海世博会毛里求斯馆
Donated by / Mauritius Pavilion of Expo 2010

毛里求斯为上海世博会特制了这枚蓝便士首日封。信封上印刷着中国 2010 年上海世博会开幕首日字样的珍贵的蓝便士邮票。

1847 年 9 月，毛里求斯总督夫人举行舞会，为邮寄请柬，当地邮局发行了两种邮票，面值分别为橘黄色 1 便士和蓝色 2 便士，图案为英国维多利亚女王侧面头像，各 500 枚。这是英国殖民地最早发行的邮票。舞会结束后，大部分请柬都被丢弃，只有十几枚邮票被一班轮船运到了欧洲和印度。目前实寄封仅发现 1 个，1993 年以 500 万美元的价格拍出。而 1 便士邮票新票存世 15 枚，2 便士新票存世 12 枚，均为世界珍邮。集合两种珍藏元素的这枚上海世博会蓝便士首日封堪称珍贵。

This Twopenny Blue First Day Cover is specially made by Mauritius for Expo 2010 Shanghai China. Twopenny blue stamps are among the rarest stamps in the world while there are only 15 new one penny stamps and 12 new two penny stamps left. This Twopenny Blue First Day Cover for Expo 2010 integrates two elements for collection and is nothing but precious.

山地大猩猩 "璋璋"
Mountain Gorilla "Zhangzhang"

捐赠方 / 上海世博会乌干达馆
Donated by / Uganda Pavilion of Expo 2010

山地大猩猩是极度濒危的物种之一，目前全球仅存不到 700 只。山地大猩猩形体巨大、相貌粗鲁，然而性情却非常温和，食草为生。目前，山地大猩猩主要生活在乌干达、刚果（金）和卢旺达三国交界地带。

乌干达一直致力于国内这一濒危动物的保护工作，保护山地大猩猩也作为其展示主题之一。馆内一共有五只山地大猩猩玩偶欢迎游客的到来，并提醒人们关注世界濒危物种。

Mountain Gorilla, with the current number of less than 700 on earth, is among the critically endangered species. Uganda has long been engaged in the protection of this endangered animal and therefore, the protection of mountain gorillas is also one of the exhibition themes.

布隆迪板雕
Burundi Plate Carving

捐赠方 / 上海世博会布隆迪馆
Donated by / Burundi Pavilion of Expo 2010

板雕与鼓是布隆迪最具代表性的工艺品。布隆迪人常将生活中庆典及劳作的情景融入板雕及手鼓的制作中。

Plate carvings and drums are the most representative crafts in Burundi. Burundians usually apply the celebrating and working scenarios to the construction of plate carvings and hand drums.

草编储物罐、篮子
Straw Woven Storage Jars and Baskets

捐赠方 / 上海世博会卢旺达馆
Donated by / Rwanda Pavilion of Expo 2010

非洲传统草编篮子及储物罐用来放置物品及食物，编织最为细密的甚至可用于盛放饮料、液体。这些草编篮子不仅是生活用品，更是非洲艺术的体现。在非洲女性充满智慧的巧手下，不必设计和绘画草样，一个个图案精美、造型匀称的篮子便可迅速制作而成。

The traditional straw woven baskets and storage jars in Africa are usually used to keep articles and food and even drinks if the weave is fine enough. These straw woven baskets are not only articles for daily use, but also an embodiment of African art.

肯特布
Kente Cloth

捐赠方 / 上海世博会加纳馆
Donated by / Ghana Pavilion of Expo 2010

肯特布发祥于西非加纳，是当地阿善提人文化的重要特征。肯特布可能是最知名的和最受欢迎的非洲纺织品。20世纪60年代肯特布甚至成为泛非运动和非洲统一运动的一种标志，一直被漂泊在外的非洲移民所使用。

肯特布通过暗色底布上亮丽的色块图案的排序来达到图样变化的效果，用经线条纹不同宽度的配置区分不同的图案。在谚语和口口相传的文化中，年长的织布工们熟记着大量的图案名称，其中一些图案名字的含义是历史事件、家庭用品、谚语或布料用途等。

Originated from Ghana in West Africa, Kente cloth is an important part of local Asante culture. Kente cloth is probably the most well-known and popular African textile, even becoming a symbol of Pan-African movement and Africa's unification movement in the 1960s.

"成人礼"仪式面具
Mask for "Coming-of-age" Ceremony

捐赠方 / 上海世博会加蓬馆
Donated by / Gabon Pavilion of Expo 2010

在加蓬的"成人仪式"上，人们会带上这种面具，身披草叶编制的服装载歌载舞，庆祝孩子的成年。

In Gabon, people wear this mask at the "coming-of-age ceremony" and costumes woven with grass leaves to sing and dance, celebrating a child's coming-of-age.

民族刀
Ethnic Knife

捐赠方 / 上海世博会吉布提馆
Donated by / Djibouti Pavilion of Expo 2010

吉布提民族刀锋利短小。刀鞘采用动物的毛皮及金属装饰。

The ethnic knife of Djibouti has a short but sharp blade. The sheath is made with animal furs and decorated with metal.

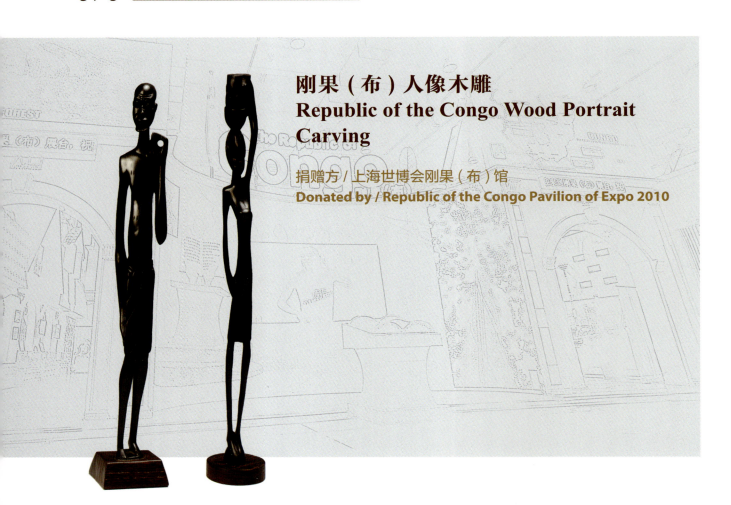

刚果（布）人像木雕
Republic of the Congo Wood Portrait Carving

捐赠方 / 上海世博会刚果（布）馆
Donated by / Republic of the Congo Pavilion of Expo 2010

草编篮子
Straw Woven Baskets

捐赠方 / 上海世博会纳米比亚馆
Donated by / Namibia Pavilion of Expo 2010

"廷嘎廷嘎"画
Tingatinga Painting

捐赠方 / 上海世博会坦桑尼亚馆
Donated by / Tanzania Pavilion of Expo 2010

著名的"廷嘎廷嘎"画是在 1960 年代由廷嘎廷嘎先生创立，以艳丽的色彩、夸张的线条和奇异的非洲元素闻名于世。

The famous "Tingatinga" painting is created by Edward Saidi Tingatinga in 1960s, well-known for bright colors, exaggerated lines and bizarre African elements.

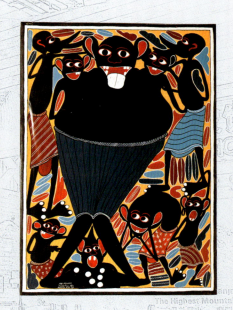

"国王守卫"木雕
Wood Carving "King's Guard"

捐赠方 / 上海世博会科特迪瓦馆
Donated by / Côte d'Ivoire Pavilion of Expo 2010

"露西"古人类化石（高仿品）
Hominine Fossil "Lucy" (replica)

捐赠方 / 上海世博会埃塞俄比亚馆
Donated by / Ethiopia Pavilion of Expo 2010

1974 年 11 月 24 日，美国古人类学家唐纳德·约翰逊和他率领的考古小组在阿法尔凹地发现了一具约 40% 完整的古人类骨骼化石。为了庆祝这一伟大的发现，唐纳德在现场播放起甲壳虫乐队的歌曲《露西在缀满钻石的天空》，并为这具 320 万岁的骨骼化石取名为"露西"。

"露西"是一具南方古猿阿法种的古人类骨骼化石，她被认为是第一个直立行走的人类，是目前所知人类的最早祖先。"露西"印证了 20 世纪人类考古学说的推断——"人类起源于非洲"。正如唐纳德·约翰逊所感慨的："某种意义上，我觉得我们发现了一个母亲。"

2010 年 5 月 13 日，埃塞俄比亚国宝——"露西"的复制品在上海世博会非洲联合馆埃塞俄比亚馆亮相。在来到上海世博会展出之前，她一直被珍藏在埃塞俄比亚国家博物馆内。

On November 24, 1974, Donald Johnson, an American paleoanthropologist, discovered a hominine fossil with 40% of the body preserved. To celebrate this great discovery, he played The Beetles' song *Lucy in the Sky with Diamonds*, and later the hominine fossil of 3.2 million years old was named after Lucy. "Lucy" confirms the inference of anthropological archaeology in the 20th century – "the human beings originate from Africa".

On May 13, 2010, a replica of "Lucy" as the national treasure of Ethiopia was displayed at Ethiopia Pavilion of African Joint Pavilion of Expo 2010 Shanghai China. Before the debut, she was treasured up in the National Museum of Ethiopia all the time.

索马里火炉
Somalia Stove

捐赠方 / 上海世博会索马里馆
Donated by / Somalia Pavilion of Expo 2010

火炉采用石头雕刻或石膏制作而成，朴实小巧。出门在外时，可携带用于在野外点火使用。

The plain and compact stove is carved out of stone or made of gypsum. It can be used to make fire outdoors when one is away from home.

女王宝座
Queen's Chair

捐赠方 / 上海世博会喀麦隆馆
Donated by / Cameroon Pavilion of Expo 2010

这把木椅为非洲部落首领的宝座，椅身的奴隶形象图案显示主人身份的高贵。非洲联合馆第一千万名游客——来自河南省的女教师吴晶坐在这把座椅上接受"一日女王"的封号，"女王宝座"由此得名。

This wooden chair is the throne for tribal leaders in Africa and the slave images on the chair show the noble status of its owner. The 1 000th visitor of African Joint Pavilion——Wu Jing, a female teacher from Henan Province——accepted the title of "One-Day Queen" sitting in this chair, and hence comes the name.

海椰子果实
Fruit of Coco de Mer

捐赠方 / 上海世博会塞舌尔馆
Donated by / Seychelles Pavilion of Expo 2010

海椰子树是塞舌尔所特有的植物，虽然名字带有"海"却并不生在海洋里。海椰子树雌雄异株合抱或并排生长，连地下的根也是相互交织在一起。更奇特的是，如果雌雄中的一株被砍，另一株便会"殉情而死"，所以海椰子树有"爱情之树"的美称。

Coco de Mer is a plant unique to Seychelles. Coco de Mer tree is dioecious while the female and male trees embrace each other or stand side by side. Even the roots underground are entwined together. More peculiarly, if one of them is cut down, the other will "die for love". Therefore, Coco de Mer trees have a reputation as "Tree of Love".

作为生物进化遗留下来的活化石，海椰子树生长速度非常缓慢，但生命力极强，可以存活千年，果实则需要七年才能成熟。成熟后的海椰子果即便随海水漂流至他处，也不能在他国的海滩上生长。

最初人们发现塞舌尔有 5 个岛上长有海椰子树，但是现在只有普拉林岛南部的"五月谷"还存有这种树种，海椰子果实变得更加珍贵，被塞舌尔视为"国宝"。1978 年，塞舌尔总统出访我国时便赠送海椰子果作为展现两国友谊的国礼。

Coco de Mer tree grows and bears fruit at a very slow pace. The ripe fruit of Coco de Mer may float to other places where it cannot grow. For this reason, the fruit of Coco de Mer is very precious and is regarded as the "National Treasure" of Seychelles.

陶瓷红花
Ceramic Red Flowers

捐赠方 / 上海世博会委内瑞拉玻利瓦尔共和国馆
Donated by / Venezuela Pavilion of Expo 2010

委内瑞拉馆内外一共有 4 500 朵这样的大红花，分别装饰其影视厅和屋顶。这种红花是在中国福建德化为上海世博会所特制的瓷器，不禁让人与委内瑞拉馆展馆那近似数字 8 的平面结构联系起来。红花的布置以循环线结构模糊淡化了层次的界限，不但加强了空间的整体感，而且平面上也丰富了层次感。

Venezuela Pavilion is decorated with altogether 4 500 ceramic red flowers which are specially manufactured in Dehua, Fujiar Province for World Expo 2010 Shanghai China. The spectacular red flowers on the outer wall of the Pavilion enhance the sense of wholeness of space and improve the sense of layers as well.

肖邦玩偶及音乐作品集
Chopard Doll and Collection of Chopin's Music

捐赠方 / 上海世博会波兰馆
Donated by / Poland Pavilion of Expo 2010

2010 年是波兰著名作曲家、钢琴家肖邦诞辰 200 周年，波兰将该年定为"肖邦年"，并在全球几十个国家举办 2 000 多场音乐会、电影、展览等活动。中国 2010 年上海世博会是波兰纪念肖邦的最重要舞台之一。

The year 2010 marked the 200th anniversary of the birth of Chopin, the famous Polish composer and pianist. Poland designated the year as the "year of Chopin" and held over 2 000 events such as concerts, movies, and exhibitions in dozens of countries around the globe. Expo 2010 Shanghai China was one of the most important stages to commemorate Chopin.

钉马蹄铁的鸡蛋
Eggs Shod with Horseshoes

捐赠方 / 上海世博会波黑馆
Donated by / Bosnia and Herzegovina Pavilion of Expo 2010

马蹄象征着吉祥幸福，鸡蛋代表生命，"马蹄铁鸡蛋"象征着生命的延续。在波黑，只有能成功地在鸡蛋壳上钉上马蹄铁的男人才有资格结婚。

Horseshoes symbolize auspiciousness and happiness, eggs symbolize life, and "eggs shod with horseshoes" represents the continuation of life. In Bosnia and Herzegovina men are not eligible to get married unless they succeed in shoeing eggshells.

南非世界杯吉祥物"扎库米"玩偶
Mascot of 2010 FIFA World Cup South Africa – Zakumi Doll

捐赠方 / 上海世博会南非馆
Donated by / South Africa Pavilion of Expo 2010

2010 年南非 FIFA 世界杯的吉祥物是一只长着一头绿色非洲卷发的可爱豹子"扎库米"。

扎库米的"生日"为 1994 年 6 月 16 日，这是南非种族隔离政策宣告结束的日子，这一天同时也是南非的"青年节"。"扎库米"名字中的头两个字母 ZA 是南非语中"南非"的缩写；后面的字母 KUMI 在许多非洲语言中的意思都是"10"，意味着南非世界杯举办的年份。在南部非洲的一些语言中，"扎库米"也有"欢迎前来"的意思。

扎库米代表了南非的人民和精神，他将伴随激动人心的世界杯比赛为人们带来欢乐。

The mascot of 2010 FIFA World Cup South Africa is a lovely African leopard with curly green hair – Zakumi. It symbolizes the people, the geography and the spirit of South Africa.

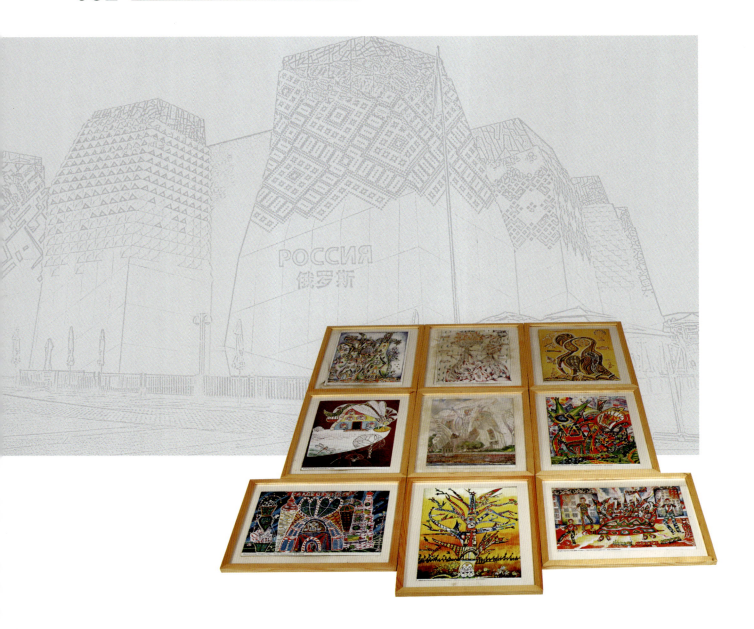

俄罗斯馆儿童画
Children's Drawings in Russia Pavilion

捐赠方 / 上海世博会俄罗斯馆
Donated by / Russia Pavilion of Expo 2010

俄罗斯馆的主题"最好的城市应该是最受孩子们喜爱的城市"是由前苏联著名儿童文学家尼古拉·诺索夫提出，俄罗斯馆内部的设计理念就来源于诺索夫的作品《小无知历险记》。展馆营造出一个美丽、精湛、充满童话色彩的儿童花园城堡，并悬挂了当地儿童绘画来演绎这一主题。

Both the theme and exhibition design of Russia Pavilion originated from the works of Николáй Нóсов, a famous writer of literature for children of former Soviet Union, and they constructed a fascinating and exquisite castle garden for children. Theme drawings by local children were hung in the pavilion.

法老时代雕塑（复制品）
Sculptures in Pharaonic Times (replicas)

捐赠方 / 上海世博会埃及馆
Donated by / Egypt Pavilion of Expo 2010

法老时代的雕塑 1：1 复制品，包括神庙护卫、女性祭司等形象，法老时期统治阶层的形象展现了神秘古老的古埃及文明。

1:1 full-scale replicas of sculptures in pharaonic times, including the figurines of Temple Guardian and Priestess, etc, exhibit the ruling class in pharaonic times and the mysterious ancient Egyptian civilization.

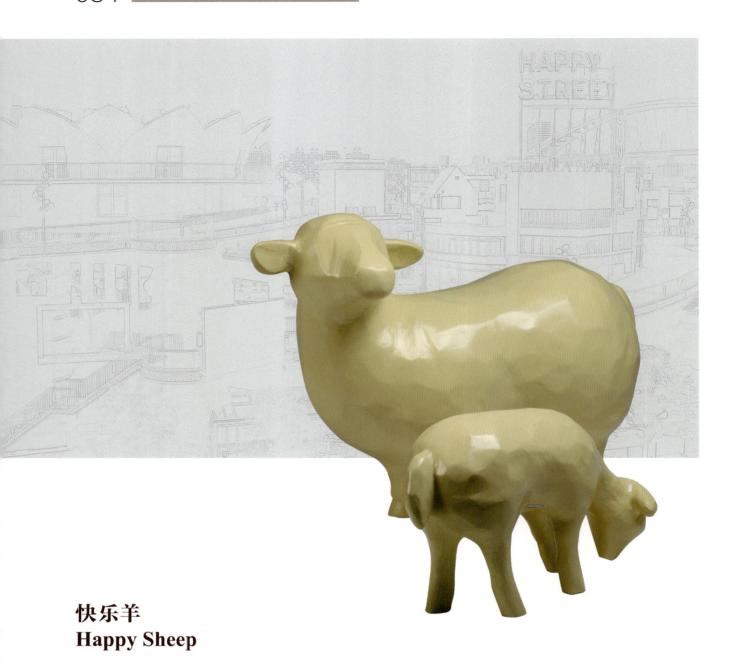

快乐羊
Happy Sheep

捐赠方 / 2010 年上海世博会荷兰王国驻上海总领事馆项目办公室
Donated by / Consulate General of the Kingdom of the Netherlands Project Office Expo 2010

快乐羊是为上海世博会荷兰馆"快乐街"度身定造。羊群站在绿色的"草地"地毯上，生动地体现了荷兰特有的牧场景象。世博期间，前往展馆参观的丹麦王妃就对这群"小动物"表达出喜爱之情。参观者们可以坐在"快乐羊"上面休息，或与之合影留念。

Happy Sheep are tailored especially for the "Happy Street" in the Netherlands Pavilion of EXPO 2010 Shanghai. The sheep flock standing on the green "grass" carpet is a vivid image of the pasture scene unique to the Netherlands.

祖母绿"海宝"
Emerald Carving of Haibao

捐赠方 / 上海世博会哥伦比亚馆
Donated by / Colombia Pavilion of Expo 2010

祖母绿宝石不仅是哥伦比亚的国石，更是哥伦比亚的象征和骄傲。专门为上海世博会打造的大小两件祖母绿宝石海宝是哥伦比亚馆的镇馆之宝。

Emerald is not only the national stone of Columbia, but also the symbol and pride of Colombians. The two emerald carvings of Haibao of different sizes made especially for Expo 2010 Shanghai China are the key highlights of the collections of Colombia Pavilion.

民族传统陶瓷艺术品
Traditional National Ceramic Artworks

捐赠方 / 上海世博会秘鲁馆
Donated by / Peru Pavilion of Expo 2010

上海世博会秘鲁馆通过独特的工艺品、首饰、民族服装及图腾雕塑展示了这个国度所拥有的独特民族文化。

Peru Pavilion of Expo 2010 Shanghai China showed the unique national culture of Peru through distinctive artworks, jewelry, national costumes and totem sculptures.

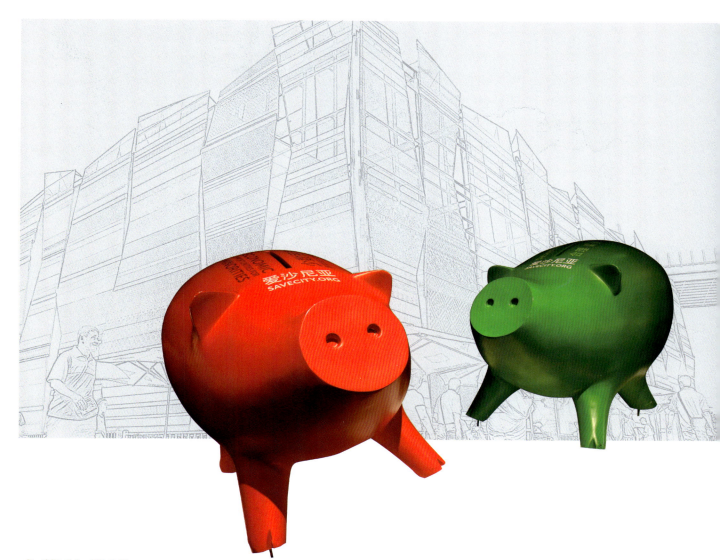

小猪储蓄罐
Piggy Bank

捐赠方 / 上海世博会爱沙尼亚馆
Donated by / Estonia Pavilion of Expo 2010

在爱沙尼亚馆，小猪形状的储蓄罐散布在展区各个角落，这 32 只有编号的小猪，分别对应 32 个城市问题，涵盖城市环境、衣食住行、教育就业、社会保障、城市规划与决策民主、资本和劳动力流动等方面，这些问题是经专家讨论选出，也是爱沙尼亚人最关心的。参观者可以选填各自最关注的问题，写下具体建议投进储蓄罐。这些建议将被保留在数据库，形成一个关于城市各类问题的报告，为寻求未来城市发展的解决之道提供帮助。

In Estonia Pavilion, 32 piggy banks which correspond respectively to 32 urban problems scattered in different corners of the exhibition area. Visitors are invited to write down specific suggestions to solve the problems and put them into the piggy banks. The suggestions will be stored in a database for the compiling of a report on various urban problems, so as to solicit help in seeking after solutions to future urban development.

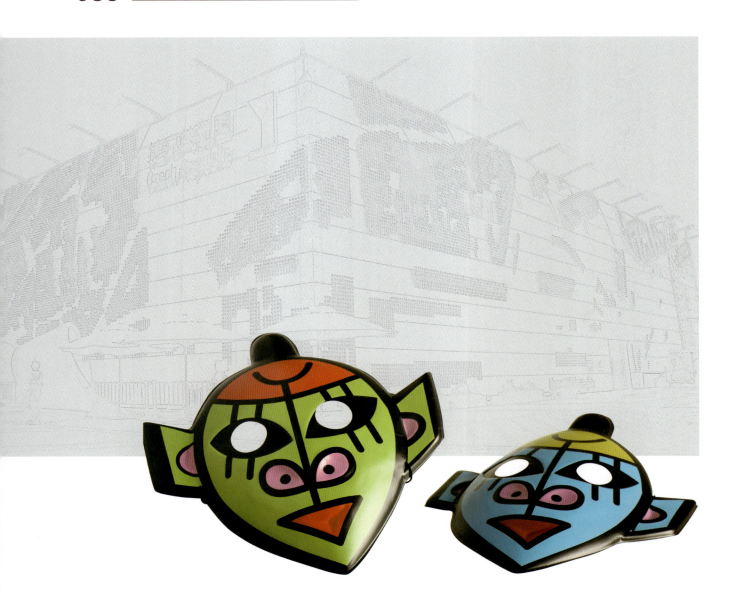

"美猴王" 面具
"Monkey King" Mask

捐赠方 / 上海世博会捷克馆
Donated by / Czech Pavilion of Expo 2010

捷克的美猴王，其形象来自捷克画家兹德涅克·斯科纳为 1960 年在捷克出版的《美猴王》所绘制的插图。这些插图的最初灵感来源于斯科纳在北京观看的京剧，在此基础上，他又融合了中国汉代画像、京剧脸谱、服饰甚至当时中国人的生活图像等多种素材，创造出对吴承恩笔下美猴王形象的一种全新阐释。

The image of the Monkey King of Czech originates from the illustrations drawn by Czech painter Zdenek Sklenar for The Monkey King published in Czech in 1960. The illustrations combine various kinds of materials, such as facial make-up of Chinese Peking Opera, into a brand-new interpretation of the image of the Monkey King created by Wu Cheng'en in his classic masterpiece.

《生于末世》节选本
Living in the End Times (Excerpts)

捐赠方 / 上海世博会斯洛文尼亚馆
Donated by / Slovenia Pavilion of Expo 2010

由斯洛文尼亚著名作家、哲学家斯拉沃热·齐泽克为世博会斯洛文尼亚馆特别写作的《生于末世》一书的节选，全套含中、英、斯文各一册，中文版由吴冠军译。

The whole set of *Living in the End Times* was written especially for Slovenia Pavilion at the World Expo by the famous Slovene writer and philosopher Slavoj Zizek. It has 3 versions – Chinese, English and Slovenian. The Chinese version was translated by Wu Guanjun.

世界上第一本《葡汉字典》(高仿品)
The First *Portuguese Chinese Dictionary* in the World (replica)

捐赠方 / 上海世博会葡萄牙馆
Donated by / Portugal Pavilion of Expo 2010

世界上第一本葡汉词典,由耶稣会士罗明坚和利玛窦于1583至1588年间完成。字典收录了神学、航海、自然、商业、外交等领域的词汇共计3000多条。其原件现藏于耶稣会罗马档案馆。

The first *Portuguese Chinese dictionary* was compiled by two Jesuits, Michele Ruggieri and Matteo Ricci, between 1583 and 1588. The dictionary includes over 3 000 entries in different fields such as theology, navigation, nature, business, and diplomacy. Its original is now kept in the Roman Archives of the Society of Jesus.

复活节岛摩埃雕塑
Moai Statues of Easter Island

捐赠方 / 上海世博会智利馆
Donated by / Chile Pavilion of Expo 2010

复活节岛是南太平洋中的一个岛屿。1722年，荷兰西印度公司的探险家雅可布·洛加文首次发现了这个小岛，由于发现该岛这一天正好是基督教的复活节，从此这个小岛被命名为复活节岛，并为世人所知。复活节岛是世界上最与世隔绝的岛屿之一。

大约10世纪到16或17世纪，在复活节岛上生活的拉帕努伊人开始修建大量的巨型石像——摩埃。这些石像与岛民的宗教和祭祀活动有着密切的关系。岛上像这样的石像一共有近千座，每一个都重达几十吨，高数米，是岛民们用玄武岩制成的斧头加工岛上火山喷发形成的凝灰岩与火山岩而成。这些巨大的石雕是如何运送到全岛各地并竖立起来的，至今仍是个谜。

Ester Island is one of the most isolated islands on earth. From about the 10th century to the 16th or the 17th century, the Rapa Nui people living on the island started to make a lot of giant stone statues – Moai. These statues were closely related with religious activities and sacrificial rites of the islanders. On the island there are nearly 1 000 such stone statues and each of them weighs dozens of tons. How these giant stone statues were transported and erected on the island remains a mystery till now.

瑞士馆登山缆车及太阳能电池板
Cable Cars and Solar Cell Panels in Swiss Pavilion

捐赠方 / 上海世博会瑞士馆
Donated by / Swiss Pavilion of Expo 2010

在上海世博会上，瑞典馆从展馆顶部盘旋而出的缆车和馆外璀璨夺目的红色"闪光"外衣都为展馆带来了超高人气。

瑞士馆运用中国的阴阳原理，将缆车作为游戏元素纳入到展馆设计中。360°全景观旋转缆车带着乘客从负荷沉重的城市螺旋上升，升入展馆顶部闲适惬意的阿尔卑斯田园乡村。在这一设计理念中，缆车就是一条纽带，把瑞士馆的城市空间和自然空间连接起来。

瑞士馆的互动型智能帷幕上缀有1万颗红色太阳能电池板。这些红色半透明聚碳酸酯板被固定在帷幕的网眼上。每个电池板都是一个独立的光电媒质，包含了一套芯片、存储盘和LED照明系统。当游客举起相机留影时，闪光灯的光能被转化为电能发出点点闪光，作为对游客拍照的"热情回应"。

By applying the Chinese philosophy of "Yin" and "Yang", Swiss Pavilion integrates cable cars into its design as a game element. The cable cars are just a link connecting the urban space in Swiss Pavilion and the natural space outside.

The interactive and intelligent facade is a curtain dotted with 10 000 solar cell panels, each of which is an independent photoelectric medium. When tourists take photos as mementos, solar energy is transformed into electric energy to sparkle, as "passionate response" to the flashlight of tourists' cameras.

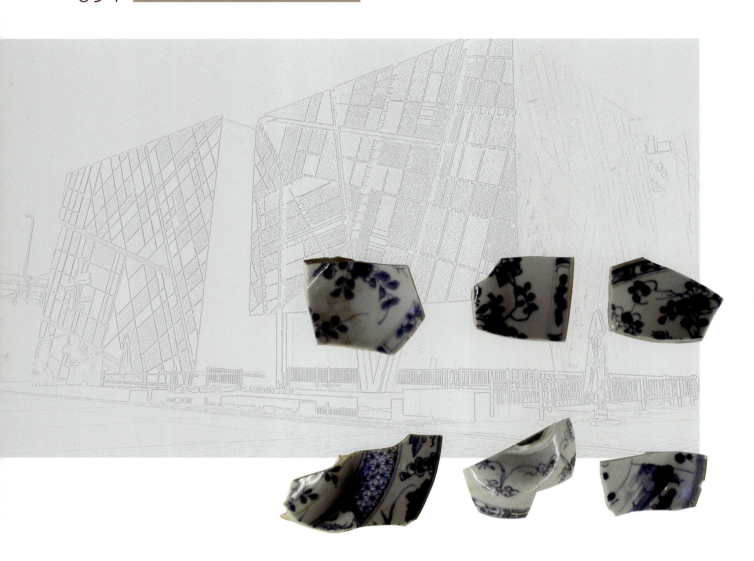

"哥德堡号"装载瓷器碎片
Porcelain Shards on "East Indiaman Gotheborg"

捐赠方 / 上海世博会瑞典馆
Donated by / Sweden Pavilion of Expo 2010

"哥德堡一号"是大航海时代瑞典著名远洋商船，曾三次航行于海上丝绸之路，并均抵达终点——中国广州，是中西方海上贸易的工具和见证。瑞典馆内展示了哥德堡号上所装载着的中国瓷器碎片。这些瓷器都是 200 多年前瑞典商人向中国专门订制的，被称为"订烧瓷"，其造型特点和用途与中国传统瓷器有很大区别，有些青花瓷在西方被用来泡咖啡和盛红酒。

上海世博会期间，复制而建的"哥德堡三号"行驶至上海黄浦江边，成为两国文化交流历史的见证。

East Indiaman Gotheborg is a tool of and witness to the marine trade between the West and the East in the Great Navigation Era. The Sweden Pavilion exhibited the Chinese porcelain shards loaded on the East Indiaman Gotheborg. All of these porcelains were ordered by Swedish businessmen and customized in China over 200 years ago. They are called "customized porcelains" and are used to make coffee and hold wine.

外墙彩色多用途模块
Multipurpose Colored Modules on External Wall

捐赠方 / 上海世博会塞尔维亚馆
Donated by / Serbia Pavilion of Expo 2010

塞尔维亚馆的外立面使用了一种多用途彩色模块。这种专利产品（Serbobox©）取材于再生性的聚丙烯塑料，其灵感来源于塞尔维亚的传统编织工艺，每一边都呈现 45 度角，组装完成后，从不同角度欣赏展馆外观，都能得到不同的感受，令整个展馆的外观充满动态。

A patented product (Serbobox©) was used for the façade of the Serbia Pavilion. The inspiration of the multipurpose colored modules sources from the traditional Serbian knitting technology. Seen from different angles, the modules, after the completion of assembly, enable visitors to experience different feelings and thus render the appearance of the pavilion extremely dynamic.

有声图书塔
Audible Book Tower

捐赠方 / 上海世博会德国馆
Donated by / Germany Pavilion of Expo 2010

书塔里收集了德国不同时期各个流派的重要文学作品。如果人们把耳朵凑近这些书，还能听到书内章节的德语及中文朗读。这些名著包括歌德的《浮士德》、君特·格拉斯的《铁皮鼓》、卡特琳·史密特的《你不会死去》、荷尔德林的《塔楼之诗》等。

The book tower has a collection of important German literary works of various schools at different times, including *Faust* by Goethe, *Die Blechtrommel* by Günter Grass, *Du stirbst nicht* by Kathrin Schmidt, and Poems by Holderlin, etc.

外墙攀爬机器人
Wall-Climbing Robot

捐赠方 / 上海世博会日本产业联合馆
Donated by / Japanese Industry Pavilion of Expo 2010

日本产业联合馆的钢架外观设计上，三只攀爬自如的机器人引人注目，展示了日本在机器人制造方面的成就。

In terms of the design of steel frame appearance of Japanese Industry Pavilion, 3 freely climbing robot are quite eye-catching. They demonstrate the breakthrough in robot-making of Japan.

概念车 "叶子"
The Leaf Concept Vehicle

捐赠方 / 上海世博会上汽 – 通用馆
Donated by / SAIC-GM Pavilion of Expo 2010

作为 "2030 年的交通工具" 的概念车 "叶子"，在中国 2010 年上海世博会 "上汽集团 – 通用汽车馆" 展出和亮相。"叶子" 在设计中以电能为主要动力来源，其技术核心是自然能源转换技术，包括光电转换技术、风电转换技术、二氧化碳吸附和转换技术。

"叶子" 的出现，重新定义了车与自然环境的关系，令车成为自然链中的一环，描绘了车与自然和谐共处的美妙场景，启迪人们不断探索发现清洁、可持续的汽车新能源。

As the concept design of "vehicle in 2030", the leaf concept vehicle was exhibited in the "SAIC-GM Pavilion at World Expo 2010 Shanghai". The kernel technology of "leaf" is the technology of natural energy conversion, including optical-electric conversion technology, wind electricity conversion technology, and carbon dioxide absorption and conversion technology. The "leaf" depicts a scene in 2030 that vehicles, people and nature will be an integrated whole and harmonious co-existence in the true sense between nature and modern transportation will be realized.

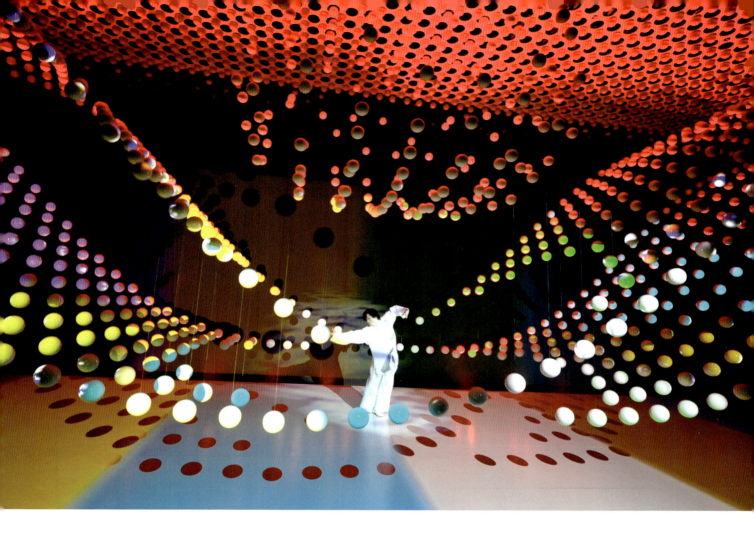

"活力矩阵"浮球
" Dynamic Matrix" Floating Balls

捐赠方 / 上海世博会民营企业联合馆
Donated by / Private Enterprises Pavilion of Expo 2010

8 分钟的"高潮秀"是上海世博会民营企业联合馆的最大看点。"千球舞太极、四季颂活力","高潮秀"演绎了四季轮回:春天,花朵争艳;夏天,海浪翻卷;秋天,麦田金黄;冬天,雪花漫天。三维浮球矩阵由 1 008 个浮球组成,结合了影像、装置、灯光、音乐和真人舞蹈。

浮球矩阵由电脑编程操控,用随着音乐起伏变幻的造型来演绎四季、歌唱生命。当太极舞者与浮球矩阵融为一体时,心随球舞,球随心动。每个浮球仿佛都是一个个生命的细胞,让人不禁联想到生命、民族、企业,都是如此繁衍变化,以至无穷。

The 8-minute-long "climax show" is the biggest highlight of Private Enterprises Pavilion of Expo 2010 Shanghai. The three-dimensional matrix of floating balls in the "climax show" is composed of 1 008 floating balls which are manipulated by computer programming. The matrix changes with the rise and fall of the tunes to demonstrate the four seasons, which reminds people of the similar circles of life, nation, and enterprises evolving and changing endlessly just like the four seasons.

青铜虎符（复制品）
Tiger-Shaped Bronze Tally (replica)

捐赠方 / 上海世博会信息通信馆
Donated by / Information and Communication Pavilion of Expo 2010

虎符是古代统治者调兵遣将用的兵符，是军事信息传递和信息认证的重要形式，体现了中国古人在信息安全方面的智慧。

虎符均由左右两片合成一只完整的虎形，内侧以阴阳榫铆扣合，外侧有完全相同的铭文，其右半由君王掌管，左半发给统领军队的将领，调动军队时由被授命的官员或使臣执虎符带往驻地，两半相符后，方可发兵。汉语中的"符合"一词便由此得来。

A tiger-shaped tally is used to move troops and dispatch generals in ancient times. It is an important way of military information transfer and authentication of message and embodies the wisdom of the Chinese ancients in information safety.

"驷马车"微缩雕塑
Miniature Sculpture of "Four-Horse Carriage"

捐赠方 / 马德里全球办公室
　　　　马德里市政厅
Donated by / Madrid Global Office
Ajuntament de Madrid

马德里是个相当适合步行漫游的城市，市内装点着各式各样的雕像、喷泉、花木和钟楼，它们各有历史典故，无声地诉说着西班牙的历史和民族文化。

上海世博会马德里案例中展示的"驷马车"微缩雕塑，展现了位于阿尔卡拉大街上的毕尔巴鄂银行总部大楼顶部的"驷马车"雕塑，原雕塑 1923 年由雕塑大师伊西里奥·德·巴斯特拉完成。

The miniature sculpture of "four-horse carriage" exhibited by the Madrid Case of Expo 2010 Shanghai China showed the four-horse sculpture on the top of the headquarters building of Bank of Bilbao located on Calle de Alcalá. The sculpture was completed by the eminent sculptor Bastera in 1923.

"伦敦为它的历史感到自豪"旅行箱
"London Loves Its History" Suitcase

提供者 / 来自 Klassnik 公司的 Tomas Klassnik
捐赠方 / 伦敦市长办公室暨伦敦发展署
Provider / Tomas Klassnik from Klassnik Corporation
Donated by / Office of the Mayor of London & London Development Agency

伦敦历史悠久，如何在未来的城市建设中充分体现伦敦人口的多样性和丰富的历史底蕴是一项挑战。上海世博会伦敦案例以"打开伦敦"为主题。古老的伦敦的旅行箱，装载着一些伦敦不为人知的历史被旅行者带往世界各个角落。

通过一个个装载着伦敦历史和现貌的旅行箱，参观者可以看到伦敦"从热爱历史到抓住机遇"的城市发展历程。

The London Case of Expo 2010 Shanghai China is themed by "Unpack London". Through the suitcases loaded with London's history and modern looks, visitors can have a glimpse of the progress of urban development of London "from loving its history to seizing opportunities".

"德成按" 蝙蝠牌匾
"Casa De Penhores Tak Seng On" —A Tablet with an Inscribed Bat

捐赠方 / 中华人民共和国澳门特别行政区政府
Donated by / Macao SAR Government, P.R.C.

上海世博会城市最佳实践区的澳门德成按案例馆按照原建筑 1 ：1 的比例兴建。其中位于地下入口处的典当业展示馆实景实物地重现了澳门典当业的发展历史，使所有参观者均感到仿佛置身于近百年前典当铺的场景中。

The Macao pawnshop "Tak Seng On" Case Pavilion in the Urban Best Practices Area of Expo 2010 Shanghai China was built at 1:1 scale of the original building. The Pawnbroking Exhibition Hall located at the underground entrance in the Pavilion reproduced the development history of pawnbroking in Macao with authentic scenes and objects.

高迪龙
Gaudi Dragon

捐赠方 / 上海世博会巴塞罗那案例馆
Donated by / Barcelona Case Pavilion of Expo 2010

酷似蛙类，又有点像蜥蜴，上海世博会巴塞罗那案例馆的徽章居然是这样一只奇怪的动物。它就是巴塞罗那标志之一的"高迪龙"。"高迪龙"是 1914 年由安东尼·高迪设计的，坐落于当地著名的奎尔公园内。

高迪是西班牙杰出的建筑天才，最具有原创精神的建筑大师，被超现实主义者奉为偶像，他的作品有东方伊斯兰、新哥特、现代主义乃至自然主义的影子，它们融合成高迪奇特的建筑风格：流动着万物的生机，对自然、生命和神的虔诚。

巴塞罗那市市长表示：选择"高迪龙"参展上海世博会，是因为它是巴塞罗那城市建筑和现代化的象征，很多中文书籍都以它作为封面，足见其形象已经深入人心。龙也是中国传统文化的重要组成部分，希望巴塞罗那的"龙"给中国人民带来吉祥好运。

Designed by Antoni Gaudi in 1914, "Gaudi Dragon" is located in the famous Park Guell in Barcelona.

Gaudi was an eminent architectural genius and a surrealistic architect master and a vanguard for innovation in Spain. The mayor of Barcelona said that the reason why "Gaudi Dragon" was selected to be exhibited at Expo 2010 Shanghai China is that it is the symbol of urban architecture and modernization of Barcelona. Dragon is also an important element of traditional Chinese culture. The "Dragon" of Barcelona will certainly bring the Chinese people auspiciousness and good luck.

毕尔巴鄂风景壁画
Bilbao Landscape Mural

捐赠方 / 上海世博会毕尔巴鄂案例馆
Donated by / Bilbao Case Pavilion of Expo 2010

毕尔巴鄂这座不为中国公众熟知的西班牙小城，却一举击败纽约、伦敦、墨尔本等 77 个城市，荣膺首届"李光耀世界城市奖"。与其他建筑奖不同的是，这个被誉为"城市界的诺贝尔"的奖项更看重城市的宜居程度以及永续性的活力。

毕尔巴鄂案例馆利用城市物理空间和社会空间的相互关系，描述了市政当局以推进物理改造来改善市民生活，提高城市形象的举措。历经 30 年，毕尔巴鄂从一座环境问题严重、工业结构陷入危机的城市，转变为欧洲生活、旅游、投资条件最好的城市之一。

上海世博会毕尔巴鄂案例馆为参展中国 2010 年上海世博会特制风景壁画，限量印制 50 件。

Although unfamiliar to the Chinese people, Bilbao, a Spanish city, is the one to be awarded the first "Lee Kuan Yew World City Prize". Over 30 years, Bilbao transformed from a city suffering from adverse environment and crisis in industrial structure to one of the cities boasting the most attractive conditions of life, tourism and investment in Europe.

"不来梅四个音乐家"雕塑
"Bremen Town Musicians" Sculpture

捐赠方 / 德国不来梅州市政府
Donated by / Bremen's Municipal Government, Germany

在不来梅市政厅左侧，摆放着一尊 1951 年由德国知名艺术家格哈德·玛克斯（Gerhard Marcks）打造的铜制雕塑，铜像讲述的是格林童话中"不来梅城市音乐家"的故事。

"不来梅四个音乐家"的童话故事充满想象力，其背后包含着"爱与困境"的主题。故事中的动物们身处逆境却仍保持乐观，团结友爱，感染着听到这个童话的人们。

上海世博会城市最佳实践区内的不来梅案例馆内，市政厅内"四个音乐家"雕塑的 1：1 模型雕塑远渡重洋来到了上海，成为馆内的"导游"。

On the left side of Bremen Town Hall stands a copper sculpture created by the renowned German artist Gerhard Marcks in 1951. The sculpture depicts the story of "Die Bremer Stadtmusikanten" in Grimm's Fairy Tales, implying the theme of "love and plight". The sculpture of "Four Musicians" in Bremen Case of Expo 2010 Shanghai China is a 1:1 replica of the original.

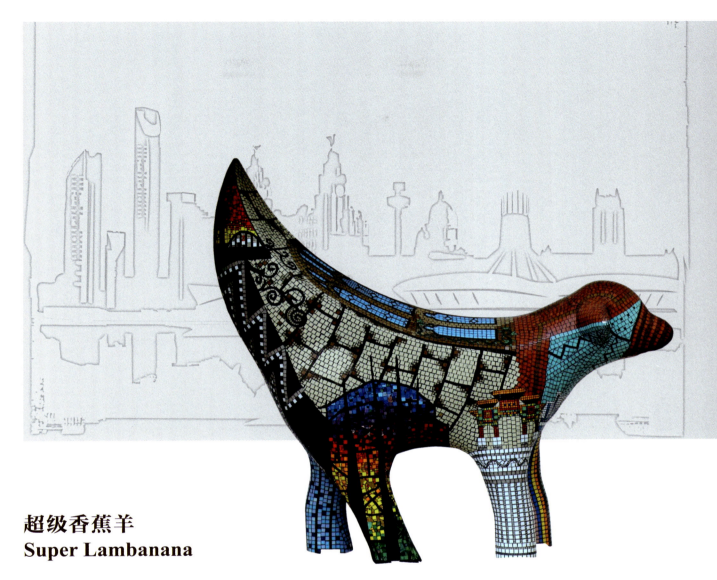

超级香蕉羊
Super Lambanana

捐赠方 / 英国利物浦市政厅
Donated by / Liverpool City, UK

超级香蕉羊是一个拥有羊的头部、香蕉形状的尾巴的艺术品，是英国港口城市利物浦 2008 年欧洲文化之都的一个标志，并作为利物浦的代表出现在 2010 年上海世博会利物浦案例馆的门口。这只"四不像"由混凝土和钢筋组成，身高 17 英尺，浑身装饰着华丽的马赛克式的色彩，可爱而又奇异的外形，令人印象深刻。

香蕉羊由日本艺术家千惠藏太郎在 1998 年创造，样子是香蕉与羊的合体，一共制作了 120 只香蕉羊，每一只都拥有独特的图案和名字。这一设计是为了激起人们对利用科技修改食品基因及成分以延长保质期的危险性的讨论，因此，雕塑引起了争议与关注。同时，香蕉羊反映了利物浦一直以来在羔羊出口及香蕉进口贸易上的悠久历史。

Super Lambanana, an artwork with the head of a lamb and a tail shaped like a banana, stands as the representative of Liverpool at the entrance to the Liverpool Case Pavilion of Expo 2010 Shanghai China. Super Lambanana was created by Japanese artist Taro Chiezo in 1998. The design aimed at triggering discussion on the danger of modifying gene and composition of foods by means of science to prolong their quality guarantee period.

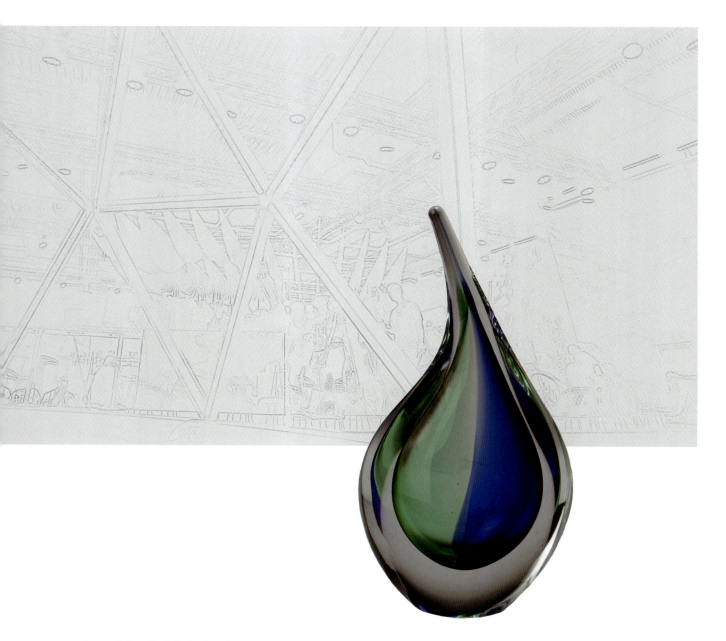

"一滴水晶"琉璃
"Crystal Drop" Colored Glaze

捐赠方 / 上海世博会鹿特丹案例
Donated by / Rotterdam Case Pavilion of Expo 2010

鹿特丹琉璃工匠所制作的水滴状琉璃工艺品。

It is a water-drop-shaped artwork of colored glaze made by craftsmen of Rotterdam.

2008 年北京奥运会吉祥物福娃
Mascots of Beijing 2008 Olympic Games – Fuwa

捐赠方 / 上海世博会北京馆
Donated by / Beijing Pavilion of Expo 2010

北京奥运会吉祥物福娃 "贝贝"、"晶晶"、"欢欢"、"迎迎" 和 "妮妮"。五个娃娃的名字连在一起便是北京对世界的盛情邀请——"北京欢迎你"。

They are five mascots of Beijing Olympic Games, Beibei, Jingjing, Huanhuan, Yingying, and Nini. Together the names form the sentence of "Beijing huanying ni" which means "Welcome to Beijing", a gracious invitation from Beijing to the world.

杨柳青年画
Yangliuqing New Year Pictures

捐赠方 / 天津市参加 2010 年上海世博会组委会办公室
Donated by / The Organizing Committee Office of Tianjin for Participation in Expo 2010

杨柳青年画为木版印绘制品，与苏州桃花坞年画并称"南桃北柳"。

上海世博会天津馆所展示的年画《莲年有余》，画面上的娃娃"童颜佛身，戏姿武架"，怀抱鲤鱼，手拿莲花。年画取其谐音，寓意生活富足，已成为年画中的经典，广为流传。

Yangliuqing New Year pictures are made by woodblock printing. In the New Year picture *Prosperity Carps*, a child is holding a carp in his arms and a lotus flower in his hand, symbolically representing an affluent life. It has become a classic image of New Year picture.

衡水内画壶
Hengshui Inside-Painted Bottle

捐赠方 / 河北省参加 2010 年上海世博会办公室
Donated by / The Organizing Committee Office of Hebei Province for Participation in Expo 2010

内画壶是清代末年发展起来的一种中国工艺品，最开始只是为了装饰鼻烟壶。

壶体一般瓶身扁平，以便有两个平面可供作画。工匠用一种特制的小竹笔从壶口伸入，倒着在瓶子里作画，需要非常高超的技艺。内画壶刚流入西方时，人们根本不相信壶内的画是手工绘制的，对其制作方法百思不得其解。

中国内画壶在 1915 年巴拿马太平洋博览会获奖，蜚声中外。

Inside-painted bottle is a kind of Chinese artwork developed in late Qing Dynasty. At first inside painting was just for decorating snuff bottles and gradually inside-painted bottles developed into a unique craft. Chinese inside-painted bottle was awarded a prize at the 1915 Panama-Pacific International Exposition and thus became famous at home and abroad.

山西门楼
Shanxi Archway

捐赠方 / 山西省世博会组委会
Donated by / The Organizing Committee of Shanxi Province for Participation in Expo 2010

山西馆门楼设计来源于山西晋祠博物院对越牌坊，以中国传统斗拱为建筑结构。门楼入口牌匾中间"山西"二字采用魏碑体。两侧挑檐上，金龙翘首；红色立柱前更有"狮敲喜鼓"。

山西门楼是中国古老建筑技巧与现代工艺的完美演绎，表现出当地传统建筑的厚重而不失精细、高大又兼具雅趣的独特风格。

The design of the archway of Shanxi Pavilion sources from the Duiyue Paifang (a traditional Chinese architectural gating style as an arch) of Jinci Museum in Shanxi Province whose architectural structure is traditional Chinese Dougong (a unique structural element of interlocking wooden brackets in traditional Chinese architecture). Archway is the perfect embodiment of ancient Chinese architectural technique and modern workmanship, representing the unique style of traditional Shanxi architecture: dignified while exquisite, and tall while elegant.

上海世博会纪念展 中华智慧展厅 "中华门楼"展项
Shanxi Archway in Commemoration Exhibition of Expo 2010

儿童砂砖画
Children's Concrete Brick Painting

捐赠方 / 上海世博会内蒙古馆
Donated by / Inner Mongolia Pavilion of Expo 2010

儿童砂砖画共有 2 010 块，组合成为上海世博会内蒙古馆的砂砖展示墙。砂砖上的图画是由草原上的孩子们亲手描绘的心中"未来的草原城市"。

The children's concrete brick painting consists of 2 010 concrete bricks which together form the display wall of concrete bricks of the Inner Mongolia Pavilion of Expo 2010 Shanghai China. The pictures on the concrete bricks were painted by the children on the prairie in person, unveiling "the future prairie city" in their mind.

满族剪纸
Manchu Paper-cutting

捐赠方 / 上海世博会吉林馆
Donated by / Jilin Pavilion of Expo 2010

满族剪纸始于明代，是满族传统文化中一个重要部分。满族民间艺人把长白山区的自然风貌、生产习俗、节令习俗、婚丧习俗及民间传说都剪成作品，装饰幸福美满的生活。

Dating from the Ming Dynasty, Manchu paper-cutting is an important part of traditional Manchu culture. Folk artisans integrate the natural landscape, production customs and folklore of Changbai Mountains into paper-cuts to adorn their happy life.

油画《家乡》
Oil Painting *Hometown*

捐赠方 / 中国书画艺术研究院哈尔滨分院
Donated by / Chinese Painting and Calligraphy Art Research Institute, Harbin Branch

黑龙江馆展出的油画《家乡》描绘出大雪中静谧的乡村美景，勾起无数游子心中的乡愁。

The oil painting *Hometown* exhibited in Heilongjiang Pavilion depicts the quiet and beautiful landscape of the countryside in heavy snow, which triggered deep homesickness of numerous people traveling far away from home.

辑里湖丝
Jili Silk

捐赠方 / 上海世博会浙江馆
Donated by / Zhejiang Pavilion of Expo 2010

南浔——清末中国最富庶的江南古镇（今属浙江省湖州市），有"辑里湖丝"故乡的美誉。

1851 年，在英国伦敦举办的首届世界博览会上，我国由上海商人徐荣村寄去的 12 包"荣记湖丝"参展。起初，包装朴实的湖丝不受青睐。而在世博会即将结束之际，湖丝仍然簇新质佳，如同刚刚运抵，一举获得我国首枚世博会金奖。

Nanxun, currently known as Huzhou, Zhejiang Province, is reputed as the hometown of "Jili Silk". At the first World Expo held in London, Britain in 1851, Xu Rongcun, a Shanghai businessman mailed a dozen packages of "Rong's Huzhou Silk" to join the exhibition and won the first World Expo Gold Award of China at the first try.

大别山红宝石石雕"红梅迎春宫扇"
Dabie Mountain Ruby Stone Carving
"Mandarin Fan of Red Plum Blossoms Greeting Spring"

捐赠方 / 王世年
      上海世博会安徽馆
Donated by / Wang Shinian
      Anhui Pavilion of Expo 2010

"红梅迎春宫扇"取材于大别山含红宝石的黑云母二长片麻岩。根据天然的纹路雕刻而成的红梅,刚强中略显妩媚。细腻雕琢的枝桠向上延伸,呈现出蓬勃向上之势。

Biotite two-feldspar gneiss containing ruby from Dabie Mountains is selected as the material for the "Mandarin Fan of Red Plum Blossoms Greeting Spring". The red plum blossoms carved following the natural grains of the rock show a rigid yet slightly enchanting posture.

白瓷雕塑"春满人间"
White Porcelain Sculpture
"Spring Reigns Everywhere"

捐赠方 / 许瑞峰
　　　　上海世博会福建馆
Donated by / Xu Ruifeng
　　　　Fujian Pavilion of Expo 2010

福建德化与江西景德镇和湖南醴陵齐名，是中国三大古瓷都之一。德化瓷器中又以白瓷最为著名，有"中国白"之美誉。

"春满人间"白瓷雕塑出自福建省工艺美术大师许瑞峰之手。瓷塑中的仙女脚踏祥云，仪态万方，双手将一只花篮举过头顶，欲将篮内的鲜花撒向人间。

Dehua County in Fujian Province is known as one of the three ancient porcelain capitals in China. Among Dehua porcelains, white porcelains are the most famous. The white porcelain sculpture "Spring Reigns Everywhere" was created by Xu Ruifeng, a master of arts and crafts from Fujian Province. The fairy maiden with divine grace is about to scatter fresh flowers to the world.

江西馆瓷器
Porcelains in Jiangxi Pavilion

捐赠方 / 江西省参与 2010 年上海世博会组委会办公室
Donated by / The Organizing Committee Office of Jiangxi Province for Participation in Expo 2010

仿乾隆青花缠枝莲寿桃纹象耳扁瓶（高仿品）
Imitation of Blue and White Flat Bottle with Interlocking Branches of Lotus, Longevity Peach Pattern and Elephant-Shaped Handles made in the Reign of Qianlong (replica)

瓷瓶瓶小口圆、唇细直颈扁腹、椭圆形式宽圈足，颈肩部有两大象衔灵芝作耳。器形设计巧妙规整，前后腹绘制青花缠枝莲纹，腹中心绘有蝠桃文，画工精湛。器底有青花"大清乾隆年制"六字篆书款，原品属清代乾隆朝御窑瓷珍品之一。

The porcelain bottle features ingenious shape design and exquisite painting. On the bottom of the bottle are six seal characters meaning "made during the reign of Qianlong in Grand Qing Dynasty". The bottle is one of the treasures made by the imperial kiln during the reign of Qianlong in the Qing Dynasty.

仿宣德青花鱼莲纹罐（高仿品）
Imitation of Blue and White Jar with Design of Fish and Lotus made in the Reign of Xuande (replica)

在中国的传统中，因"鱼"与"余"谐音，鱼寄托了中国人对富裕美满的希望。鱼纹罐早在宋代就盛极一时。青花鱼罐所绘鱼纹与枝叶曼妙的萍藻莲花，均为宣德时期官窑的青花盘上常见的图案。宣德青花鱼莲纹罐在中国瓷器制造史上起着承上启下的作用。

Both the fish patterns and exquisite branches and leaves of duckweed and aquatic plants painted on the blue and white jar were common patterns on the blue and white dishes made in the imperial kiln during the reign of Xuande in the Ming Dynasty. They play the role of a connecting link between the preceding and the following in the history of porcelain making in China.

仿宣德青花鹦鹉寿桃盘（高仿品）
Imitation of Blue and White Dish with Design of Parrots and Longevity Peaches Made in the Reign of Xuande (replica)

瓷盘圈足内细砂底，器形规整大方，胎质坚硬莹白。盘壁绘连枝灵芝纹，盘心描绘有鹦鹉及寿桃，内壁绘有折枝花果，纹样细腻逼真，白釉肥润，青花典雅。宣德青花鹦鹉寿桃盘为明宣德年间同类器中规格较大的品种，该类瓷器保存完整者极为少见。

There are parrots and longevity peaches painted at the center of the porcelain dish and flowers and fruit on its inner wall. The dish is of a bigger size among the same kind of porcelains during the reign of Xuande in the Ming Dynasty. Such porcelains kept intact are very rare.

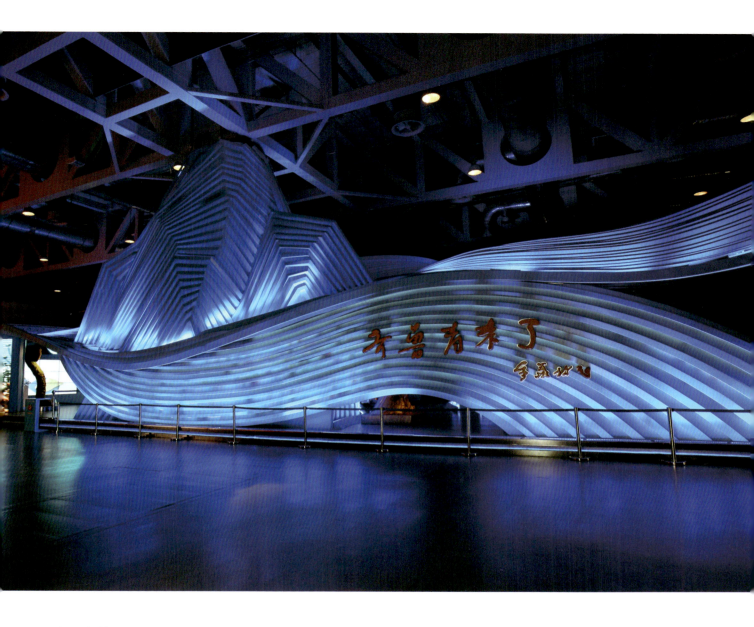

孔子像
Statue of Confucius

捐赠方 / 山东省人民政府
Donated by / Shandong Provincial People's Government

孔子（前551年—前479年），名丘，字仲尼，春秋末期鲁国陬邑（今山东省曲阜市东南）人。中国古代文学家、思想家、政治家、教育家，儒家学派创始人。

上海世博会举办期间，正值孔子诞辰2 561周年。为纪念孔子，上海世博会山东馆内展示的金色孔子像高度为2.561米。雕像神态和蔼、双手作揖，向每一个前来参观的游客传达"有朋自远方来，不亦乐乎"的精神。

Confucius (551–479 B.C.) was a litterateur, thinker, statesman, educator and the founder of Confucian school in ancient China. The year 2010 in which Expo 2010 Shanghai was held marked the 2 561th anniversary of the birth of Confucius.

后母戊鼎（高仿品）
Houmuwu Quadripod (replica)

捐赠方 / 河南省参与 2010 年上海世博会组委会办公室
Donated by / The Organizing Committee Office of Henan Province for Participation in Expo 2010

后母戊鼎是商王祖庚或祖甲为祭祀母亲戊而作的祭器，中国商周时期青铜器的代表作，原称"司母戊鼎"或"司母戊大方鼎"，中国国家一级文物。

"后母戊"青铜方鼎 1939 年出土于河南省安阳市武官村。鼎高 133 厘米，口长 112 厘米，口宽 79.2 厘米，重 832.84 千克，是世界上迄今出土最重的青铜器，有"镇国之宝"的美誉。

"后母戊"青铜方鼎因器腹部内壁铸有铭文"后母戊"而得名，这三个字为某位商王母亲的庙号。该鼎厚立耳（其中一耳为后配），折沿宽缘，直壁深腹平底，腹部呈长方形，下承四中空柱足。器耳上饰一列浮雕式鱼纹，首尾相接，耳外侧饰浮雕式双虎食人首纹，腹壁四面正中及四隅各有突起的短棱脊，腹部周缘饰饕餮纹，均以云雷纹为地。足上端饰浮雕式饕餮纹，下衬三周凹纹。此器形制巨大，胸围庄严，是目前所知中国先秦时期最重要的青铜器。

后母戊鼎现藏于中国国家博物馆。

Houmuwu Quadripod is a representative bronze ware in the period of the Shang and Zhou Dynasties in China and is listed as a national grade-one cultural relic.

The quadripod was unearthed in Wuguan Village, Anyang City, Henan Province in 1939. The quadripod, 832.84 kg in weight, 133 cm in height with an opening as long as 112 cm and as wide as 79.2 cm, is the heaviest bronze ware unearthed in the world by now, as well as the most important bronze ware in the pre-Qin period in China known now. It is reputed as the "National Treasure of China".

Houmuwu Quadripod is now kept in the National Museum of China.

虎座凤架鼓（复制品）

Wooden Drum with Tiger-shaped Stand and Phoenix-shaped Rack (replica)

捐赠方 / 湖北省世博办
Donated by / The Organizing Committee Office of Hubei Province for Participation in Expo 2010

虎座凤架鼓是战国时期楚国重要的乐器种类，也是楚文化的代表器物，现藏于湖北省博物馆内。虎座凤架鼓由立凤、卧虎、悬鼓和器座组成。鼓架上两只背向而踞的卧虎为底座，虎背上各立一只长腿昂首的鸣凤，背向而立的两只凤鸟中间有一面大鼓用红绳悬挂于凤冠之上。

The wooden drum with tiger-shaped stand and phoenix-shaped rack was an important kind of musical instrument of Chu State in the Warring States Period in China. The two crouching tigers facing opposite directions comprise the base of the stand and on each tiger stands a long-legged singing phoenix perking up its head. The drum is now kept in Hubei Provincial Museum.

菊花夔纹瓶
Bottle with Design of Chrysanthemum and Dragon Pattern

捐赠方 / 湖南省工艺美术研究所
Donated by / Arts and Crafts Research Institute of Hunan Province

菊花石雕是中国著名的三大石雕之一，其石质地细腻，花态逼真，白色晶莹的菊花，映衬着黑色基质岩石的底色，黑白分明，充分展现了自然造化的神奇。据史载，在 1915 年巴拿马太平洋万国博览会上，我国工艺大师戴清升携菊花石雕"映雪"花瓶和"梅、兰、竹、菊"屏风参展，一举荣获金奖，作品至今保存在联合国博物馆内。

The vivid chrysanthemum stone carving fully demonstrated the magic of the nature. According to the historical record, at the 1915 Panama-Pacific International Exposition, the craft master of China, Dai Qingsheng, participated in the expo with his chrysanthemum stone carving vase "Snow" and was awarded the gold prize. The work is still kept in the Museum of the United Nations.

潮绣《上海世博会广东馆》
"South Cantonese Culture" — Guanlan Porcelain Painting with Under-Glaze Carving

捐赠方 / 上海世博会广东馆
Donated by / Guangdong Pavilion of EXPO 2010

潮绣是广东刺绣的一种，与苏绣、湘绣、蜀绣同被誉为中国四大名绣。潮绣有绒绣、钉金绣、金绒混合绣和线绣等工艺手法。潮绣的图案严谨繁复，多运用金银线与绒线结合绣制，色彩瑰丽，层次分明立体，具有强烈的视觉效果。

Chao Embroidery is one of Cantonese embroidery style and praised as one of Four Famous Embroidery Styles in China with Su Embroidery, Xiang Embroidery and Shu Embroidery. Chao Embroidery is featured with such art craft as woolen needlepoint tapestry, cannetille thread embroidery, mixed embroidery of cannetille and floss, and thread embroidery. The precise and complicated patterns of Chao Embroidery are mainly stitched with cannetille floss combined, boasting strong visual effects with multiple bright colors and distinct gradations.

侗族风雨桥模型
Model of Wind-Rain Bridge of Dong Ethnic Group

捐赠方 / 上海世博会广西馆
Donated by / Guangxi Pavilion of Expo 2010

"侗族风雨桥"模型，桥长 270 厘米、宽 60 厘米、高 90 厘米，是完全以程阳风雨桥为原型，以 1：40 的比例精心打造，里面的构造、建造模式以及材料都与程阳风雨桥完全一样。整座模型不用一钉一铆，大小条木凿木相吻，以榫衔接，结构纵横交错却一丝不差。

The model of the "Wind-Rain Bridge of Dong Ethnic Group", with Chengyang Wind-Rain Bridge as its exact prototype, was created exquisitely at a scale of 1:40. The whole model, without using any nails or rivets and featuring a criss-cross structure, is a perfect reproduction of its prototype.

黄花梨雕"田园趣事"
Yellow Pear Wood Carving — "Pastoral Fun"

捐赠方 / 上海世博会海南馆
海南国盛家具有限公司
Donated by / Hainan Pavilion of Expo 2010
Hainan Guosheng Furniture Co., Ltd.

"田园趣事"以珍贵的黄花梨木为材料，雕刻松鼠跃动于枝头的情景。作品使用整块木料一气呵成，五只松鼠神态不同，动作各异，展现了娴熟高超的雕刻技艺，表现出闲适宁静的田园生活美景。

With the precious yellow pear wood as its material, "Pastoral Fun" created a scene of squirrels leaping about on branches. The work was completed at one stretch with a complete piece of wood. The five squirrels, with different looks and actions, show the leisure and tranquility of the idyllic life.

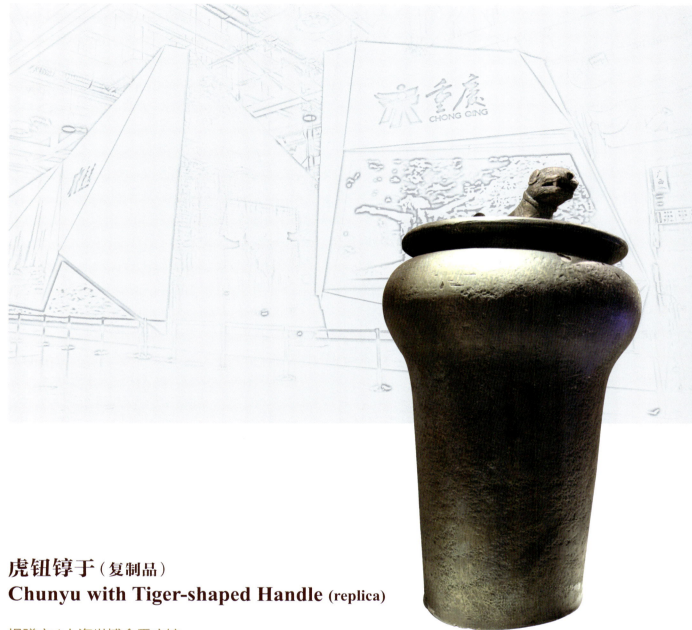

虎钮錞于（复制品）
Chunyu with Tiger-shaped Handle (replica)

捐赠方 / 上海世博会重庆馆
Donated by / Chongqing Pavilion of Expo 2010

錞于是中国古代乐器，由錞与于两种器形复合而成。春秋时期在黄河流域和长江流域都有錞于，并用于战阵。

錞于传入清江流域及三峡地区的巴人区域后，巴人逐步改变了錞于原有的特征，继承和袭用了錞于的形体和音乐功能，同时对錞于之钮加以改造创新，以虎为钮，让虎的威严凌驾于錞于之上，使之成为巴民族的象征，并以此物祈求虎神的保护。虎钮錞于是巴文化与汉文化融合的典型器物。

Chunyu is a kind of musical instrument used in ancient China to enhance troop morale in war. It combines two vessel shapes: Chun and Yu (a broad-mouthed receptacle for holding liquid). The Ba people (an ethnic group living in eastern Sichuan and western Hubei provinces in ancient China) made tiger-shaped handle for Chunyu to pray for the protection from the God of Tiger. Chunyu is a typical utensil integrating the Ba culture and the Han culture.

四川国酿
National Liquors Made in Sichuan Province

荣获 1915 年巴拿马太平洋万国博览会金奖五粮液
Wuliangye, awarded the gold prize at the 1915 Panama-Pacific International Exposition

捐赠方 / 宜宾五粮液股份有限公司
Donated by / Wuliangye Yibin Co.,Ltd.

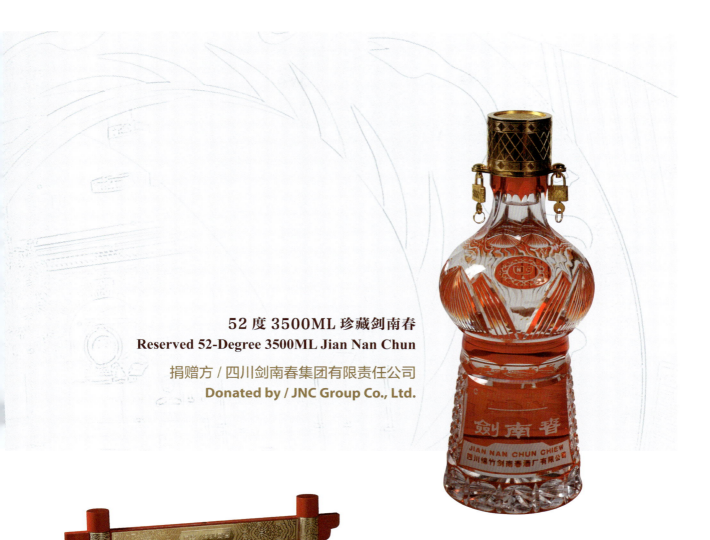

52 度 3500ML 珍藏剑南春
Reserved 52-Degree 3500ML Jian Nan Chun

捐赠方 / 四川剑南春集团有限责任公司
Donated by / JNC Group Co., Ltd.

泸州老窖纪念酒"国窖 1573"国礼酒
Memorial Liquor of Luzhou Laojiao – National Gift
"National Cellar 1573"

捐赠方 / 泸州老窖股份有限公司
Donated by / Luzhou Lao Jiao Co., Ltd.

贵州馆模型"鼓楼·银饰"
Model "Drum Tower · Silver Ornaments" in Guizhou Pavilion

捐赠方 / 贵州省委、贵州省政府
Donated by / Guizhou Central Committee of the CPC, Guizhou Provincial People's Government

贵州馆将贵州的山水自然和多元民俗文化巧妙结合，抽取风雨桥、鼓楼、苗寨、银饰和山水瀑布等极具贵州特色的视觉元素，展现了贵州生态家园之"醉"和珍物民风之"醉"。

打造上海世博会贵州馆，共使用了来自贵州本土的 300 多立方米杉木木料，这使贵州馆成为上海世博园中唯一一个用木料打造主体建筑的主题展馆。贵州馆及其模型均采用原汁原味的侗族营建工艺，不用一钉一铆搭建而成。

贵州馆模型模型以 1：15 再现展馆风貌。

Guizhou Pavilion combines natural landscapes and folk culture of Guizhou Province delicately to show folk customs of Guizhou Province. Guizhou Pavilion of Expo 2010 Shanghai China is the only pavilion whose main building is built with wood without using any nails or rivets.

牛虎铜案（复制品）
Bronze Table with Figurines of Oxen and Tiger (replica)

捐赠方 / 上海世博会云南馆
Donnor / Yunnan Pavilion of Expo 2010

牛虎铜案原品为古滇战国时期青铜材料铸成的案祭礼器，高 43 厘米，出土于江川李家山 24 号墓，是云南省博物馆镇馆之宝。

牛虎铜案反映了战国时期古滇人对自然与生活的观察和理解。器物大小搭配，塑造动静结合。其立意独具匠心、器形美观稳重，既和中原及西北青铜文化有着历史渊源，又有着鲜明的边疆民族特色，是云南青铜文化艺术的杰作。

The bronze table with figurines of oxen and tiger is a table-shaped sacrificial vessel cast in bronze in Ancient Dian Kingdom in the Warring States Period. It not only can be traced back to bronze culture in the Central Plains and Northwestern China, but also features distinct characteristics of ethnic groups around the border areas. It is a masterpiece of bronze culture and art in Yunnan Province.

《扎西德勒图——欢乐的藏历年》
Tashi Delek – Merry Tibetan New Year

捐赠方 / 西藏自治区参与 2010 年上海世博会工作领导小组办公室
Donated by / The Leading Group Office of Tibet Autonomous Region for Participation in Expo 2010

上海世博会西藏馆内的《扎西德勒图——欢乐的藏历年》壁画是根据北京人民大会堂西藏厅内的同名壁画创作的，展品以仿真喷绘手法扩大制作，颜色及表现力都与原作相当。西藏馆的艺术顾问叶星生（嘉措）先生正是人民大会堂西藏厅内《扎西德勒图》的原作者。

全图中心为吉祥双斗、羊头、青苗及各类吉祥物；周围为跳锅庄舞的藏族男女。壁画左面的中心内容为牧区妇女手举辞旧的火把，围成一圈的人们有的除夕夜沐浴，有的吃"古突"。新年初一背圣水、抛五谷、弹六弦、跳热巴舞等藏族新年活动场面跃然眼前。右面中心内容是牧区老人为迎新说唱"折嘎"，有人献哈达、跳藏戏，展现了赛马、酒歌、备耕等传统民俗风情和节庆娱乐。画的背景是布达拉宫、雪山、祥云、江水。家家团圆，欢庆藏历新年的主题在画面上洋溢开来。

The mural *Tashi Delek – Merry Tibetan New Year* in Tibet Pavilion of Expo 2010 Shanghai China was created based on the mural with the same name in the Tibet Hall, Great Hall of People in Beijing. Both the color and expressive force of the mural can rival those of the original.

The painting, which is set against the background of the Potala Palace, snow-capped mountain, auspicious clouds, and river water, express the theme of families getting together and celebrating the Tibetan New Year.

唐三彩骑骆驼乐舞俑（复制品）
Tri-colored Glazed Pottery of the Tang Dynasty
—Singing and Dancing Figurines Sitting on a Camel (replica)

捐赠方 / 上海世博会陕西馆
　　　　陕西省国际贸易促进会
Donated by / Shaanxi Pavilion of Expo 2010
　　　　China Council for the Promotion of International Trade Shaanxi Sub Council

上海世博会陕西馆展示的唐三彩骑骆驼乐舞俑高 58.4 厘米，首尾长 43.4 厘米，乐舞俑高 25.1 厘米，原器物 1957 年出土于陕西省西安市鲜于庭诲墓。

骑骆驼乐舞俑中的骆驼昂首挺立，驮载了 5 个汉、胡成年男子。中间一个胡人正载歌载舞，其余 4 人围坐演奏。他们手中的乐器仅残留一把琵琶，据夏鼐先生研究，这 4 人应该是一人拨奏琵琶，一人吹筚篥，二人击鼓，均属胡乐。唐三彩骑骆驼乐舞俑巧妙地夸张了人与驼的比例，造型优美生动，釉色鲜明润泽，代表了唐三彩的最高水平。

The tri-colored glazed pottery of the Tang Dynasty – singing and dancing figurines sitting on a camel exhibited by Shaanxi Pavilion of Expo 2010 Shanghai China shows the scene of acrobatic performance of Hu ethnic group in vogue during prosperous period in the Tang Dynasty: four musicians of Hu ethnic group holding different musical instruments sitting on a camel, festively singing and dancing. The work represents the highest level of tri-colored glazed pottery of the Tang Dynasty.

铜奔马（复制品）
Bronze Galloping Horse (replica)

捐赠方 / 甘肃省参加 2010 年上海世博会组委会
Donated by / the Organizing Committee Office of Gansu Province for Participation in Expo 2010

铜奔马原器物为东汉时期器物，又名"马踏飞燕"、"马超龙雀"，1969 年于武威市雷台汉墓出土。器物通高 34.5 厘米，长 45 厘米，宽 13.1 厘米，重 7.3 千克。

铜奔马造型矫健精美，作昂首嘶鸣、疾足奔驰状。塑造者摄取了奔马三足腾空、一足超越飞鸟的瞬间。飞鸟回首惊顾，更增强奔马疾速向前的动势，构思奇巧，奔马全身的着力点集注于超越飞鸟的一足上。工匠精确地掌握了力学平衡原理，造型精炼，铸工卓越。

铜奔马被认为是东西方文化交往的使者和象征，被确定为中国旅游的标志。

The bronze galloping horse is a utensil made in the Eastern Han Dynasty. The bronze horse is characterized by ingenious design, refined sculpt, and excellent casting. The shaper captured the instant moment of the galloping horse with three hoofs in air and the other stepping on a flying bird. The bronze galloping horse was designated as the symbol of Chinese tourism.

"三江源水献世博"水坛
Water Forum: "Water from the Source of Three Rivers Dedicated to the World Expo"

捐赠方 / 青海省商务厅
Donated by / Department of Commerce of Qinghai Province

格拉丹东雪峰融化的雪水形成了滔滔的长江，上海是长江的入海口，而青海则是长江的发源地。上海世博会青海馆的主题为"中华水塔——三江源"。青海馆将取自长江、黄河、澜沧江三江源头的圣洁之水作为特别礼物献给上海世博会。

"三江源"不仅旨在展现青海独特的地理环境，更让人们在认识、了解三江源的同时，也能对水与生命、水与城市、水与文明等主题进行进一步的思考和探讨。

The theme of Qinghai Pavilion of Expo 2010 Shanghai China is "Water Tower of China – Source of Three Waters". Qinghai Pavilion takes the holy water from the source of the three rivers – the Yangtze River, the Yellow River, and the Lancang River as a special gift for Expo 2010.

鎏金铜牛（高仿品）
Gilded Bronze Ox (replica)

捐赠方 / 上海世博会宁夏馆
Donated by / Ningxia Pavilion of Expo 2010

"鎏金铜牛"身长120厘米，宽38厘米，高45厘米，重188千克，牛身横卧，头上两角弧度优美，两眼圆睁，全身散发着柔和的金色光芒。

这件青铜铸造的牛姿态呈向前俯卧状，体态健壮，比例匀称，造型逼真，个体硕大。铜牛中空，外表通体鎏金。制作时需要将冶炼、模具雕塑、浇铸、抛光和鎏金等工艺集于一体，反映出西夏青铜铸造工艺的高超水平，是西夏艺术品中的珍品。

The whole body of the crouching "Gilded Bronze Ox" with two wide-open eyes reflects soft gold light. The casting of the bronze ox requires an integration of various crafts, such as smelting, die carving, casting, polishing and gilding, which reflects the high standard of bronze casting technique in the Western Xia Dynasty. The work is a treasure among artworks made in the Western Xia Dynasty.

"青碧玉"新疆民族乐器
"Green Jade" Musical Instruments of Ethnic Groups in Xinjiang

捐赠方 / 上海世博会新疆馆
　　　　世玉文化传播有限公司
Donated by / Xinjiang Pavilion of Expo 2010
　　Shanghai Shiyu (World Jade) Culture Communication Co., Ltd.

上海世博会新疆馆内展示的民族乐器采用青碧玉制作而成,分别为当地传统的民族乐器"都它尔"、"热瓦普"和"达卜"。

The national musical instruments exhibited in Xinjiang Pavilion of Expo 2010 Shanghai China are made of green jade. They are traditional local national musical instruments in Xinjiang Autonomous Region – "Dutor", "Rawap" and "Tabour".

"永远盛开的紫荆花"雕塑
Ever-Blooming Bauhinia Sculpture

捐赠方 / 上海世博会香港馆
Donated by / Hong Kong Pavilion of Expo 2010

"永远盛开的紫荆花"坐落于香港维多利亚湾畔,香港会议展览中心新翼前的金紫荆广场。1997年7月1日,香港特别行政区政府成立,中央人民政府将一座金紫荆雕塑"永远盛开的紫荆花"作为贺礼赠送给香港特别行政区政府。

"永远盛开的紫荆花"根据象征香港的紫荆花含苞待放的形状雕刻而成。它以青铜铸造,表面贴着金箔,并用暖红色的花岗岩基座承托。原雕塑重70吨,长、宽、高均为6米,花朵部分高3.5米。基座圆柱方底,寓意九州方圆,环衬的长城图案象征祖国永远拥抱着香港。底座上刻有"永远盛开的紫荆花",象征着香港永远繁荣昌盛。

Located on the Golden Bauhinia Square in front of Hong Kong Convention and Exhibition Centre New Wing, *Ever-Blooming Bauhinia* is a gift to Hong Kong SAR Government from the Central People's Government to celebrate Hong Kong's return to China on July 1, 1997. The *Ever-Blooming Bauhinia* was carved based on the shape of a budding bauhinia symbolizing Hong Kong. The sculpture symbolizes the ever-prosperity of Hong Kong.

"玉兔宫灯"
"Jade Rabbit Lantern"

捐赠方 / 中华人民共和国澳门特别行政区
Donated by / Macao SAR, China

宫灯根据上海世博会澳门馆的"玉兔宫灯"外型进行设计。

澳门馆设计灵感来自中国华南地区古时的兔子灯笼，寓意"和谐相容"和"机灵通达"。外层以双层玻璃薄膜为材料，全透明的结构寓意开放的和谐社会。

The shape of the palace lantern was the same as that of the "Jade Rabbit Lantern" of the Macao Pavilion of Expo 2010 Shanghai China. The design of the Macao Pavilion was inspired by the rabbit lanterns popular in South China in ancient times, implying "harmony" and "smartness".

"心灯"纪念徽章及茶具
"Lantern of Heart" Commemorative Badges and Teaware

捐赠方 / 上海世博会台湾馆
Donated by / Taiwan Pavilion of Expo 2010

台湾馆的设计概念来自"孔明灯",台湾馆的主题为"山水心灯——自然·心灵·城市"。依照台湾民间传统习俗,凡重要节庆皆会通过放孔明灯来祈求平安幸福,因此台湾馆运用此设计理念来传达祈福许愿与净化心灵的愿望。台湾馆希望通过孔明灯,让参观民众能为己,亦能为社会、为世界齐心祈福,也向世人展现台湾人民充满大爱的心灵。

The design concept of the Taiwan Pavilion originates from "Kong Ming Lantern", which implies to deliver the message of love from Taiwan to the world. It is the intent of Taiwan Pavilion that the visitors can be of one heart to pray together not only for themselves, but for the society and the world.

上海世博会博物馆
藏品捐赠

Collectibles Donation for World Expo Museum

一、藏品征集范围

上海世博会博物馆藏品征集活动面向世博会所有官方和非官方参展者、办博企事业单位、社会各界世博爱好者及收藏者。

国际展览局希望每一届世博会都能留下一份记忆，无论大小，无论经济价值的高低，每一件征集到的藏品都将作为今后展示世界博览会的重要展陈元素。

1. 文献资料

世博会博物馆接收的文献资料包括：

（1）生动演绎世博会主题的资料；

（2）世博会展馆设计理念的资料；

（3）活动、论坛成果；

（4）世博会相关出版物等。

2. 实物藏品

世博会博物馆接收的实物藏品包括：

（1）世博会广受欢迎的核心展品；

（2）与世博会主题相关的藏品；

（3）突出民族性、文化独特性的藏品等。

二、捐赠回报

为感谢捐赠方对世博会博物馆的大力支持，对于捐赠方及其赠送的实物藏品，世博会博物馆将给予以下回报：

1. 由世博会博物馆为捐赠者出具《捐赠证书》；

2. 捐赠者及实物藏品在世博会博物馆展示及对外推广中，享有署名权；

3. 以世博会博物馆宣传册刊名纪念、举行仪式等多种形式进行推广回报，具体形式由双方协商。

三、捐赠须知

1. 捐赠的物品必须具有合法性，捐赠者必须拥有捐赠品的所有权，并需签署文件以兹证明；

2. 世博会博物馆将根据馆藏规定和其他客观因素，决定会否将捐赠的物品收编为馆藏；

3. 世博会博物馆全权拥有该（批）收编物品的所有权、使用权、版权和外借权等；

4. 捐赠藏品中涉及进境物资的，捐赠者应在实物藏品移交之前，和世博会博物馆共同办妥相关清关手续；

5. 世博会博物馆保留所有有关藏品征集的解释权。

What Will Likely Be Collected by World Expo Museum

The collection of the World Expo Museum is open for all Expo official and unofficial participants, sponsoring enterprises and public institutions and fans and collectors from all walks of life.

The Bureau of International Exhibitions (BIE) hopes that the memory of each World Expo can be kept. And every collected piece, regardless of its size and value, will be treated as an important exhibit to fully display World Expo.

Archieves

World Expo Museum will be happy to receive archieves including:

a) documents for development of Expo themes;

b) documents showing design philosophy of the Pavilions;

c) documents recording achievements of the events and forums;

d) Expo—related publications, etc.

Collectibles

World Expo Museum will be happy to receive collectibles including:

a) core and popular exhibits at the Expo;

b) collectibles related to Expo themes;

c) collectibles with strong ethnic and cultural particularity.

Rewards for The Donation

In order to show our gratitude, World Expo Museum will reward donators in following ways:

a. World Expo Museum will award a certificate of donation to the donator;

b. The donators will have the right of authorship when their donated exhibits are displayed in the Museum or promoted elsewhere;

c. Donators will be mentioned in the pamphlets of World Expo Museum, or a donating ceremony will be held. The donators can negotiate with the Museum on the particular rewarding way.

Notice for Donators

a. The objects to be donated must be lawfully possessed and owned by the donators, which should be certified with signing of relevant documents;

b. World Expo Museum has the final say over whether the donated objects will be listed among the permanent collection of the museum or not in accordance with the regulations governing the collection of items at the Museum and other concrete conditions;

c. After the donation, World Expo Museum will be in possession of the following rights concerning the donated objects: ownership, rights of use, copyrights and lending rights.

d. Where the donated exhibits have to go through customs supervision, the donators shall cooperate with World Expo Museum for customs clearance before the collectibles are transferred;

e. World Expo Museum retains the final say over the interpretation of how the collectibles should be collected.

世博会，一个人类文明交流的盛会；

World Expo is a grand event for communications of human civilizations;

您的宝贵捐赠，将为世博会的美好留下永久记忆。

Your precious donation will leave a permanent mark in promoting the Expo.

世博会，一个人类文化沟通的舞台；

World Expo is a platform for the exchanges of human cultures;

您的慷慨捐赠，将让我们后代了解世博会的永恒辉煌。

Your generous donation will enable our children to understand the glory of Expo.

世博会博物馆承诺：

World Expo Museum hereby pledges that:

每一份捐赠品，都将成为世博会历史的永久记忆！

Every donated object will be remembered forever in the history of the World Expo!

图书在版编目（CIP）数据

上海世博会博物馆馆藏精品（一）/上海世博会博
物馆 编. ——上海：东方出版中心，2013.4
　　ISBN 978-7-5473-0575-1

　Ⅰ.①上… Ⅱ.①上… Ⅲ.①博览会—博物馆—陈列
品—上海市—2010 Ⅳ.①G269.275.1

中国版本图书馆CIP数据核字(2013)第067175号

责任编辑：沈　　敏
装帧设计：董　　伟
技术编辑：尚小平

上海世博会博物馆馆藏精品（一）

出版发行：东方出版中心
地　　　址：上海市仙霞路345号
电　　　话：021—62417400
邮政编码：200336
经　　　销：全国新华书店
印　　　刷：上海中华商务联合印刷有限公司
开　　　本：889×1194毫米　1/16
字　　　数：100千字
印　　　张：12
插　　　页：4
版　　　次：2013年4月第1版第1次印刷
ISBN 978-7-5473-0575-1
定　　　价：168.00元